MR. & MRS. SUNDAY'S
SUPPERS

LORRAINE WALLACE
MR. & MRS. SUNDAY'S
SUPPERS

HOUGHTON MIFFLIN HARCOURT
BOSTON · NEW YORK

To Mr. Sunday and
Our Beautiful Family

Text copyright © 2015 by Lorraine Wallace
Photographs copyright © 2015 by Waterbury Publications. Inc.
Additional photographs (pages 4–6, 9, 11–14, 17, 19)
copyright © 2015 by Yassine El Mansouri

For information about permission to reproduce selections
from this book, write to Permissions, Houghton Mifflin Harcourt Publishing Company, 215 Park Avenue South, New York,
New York 10003.

www.hmhco.com

Library of Congress Cataloging-in-Publication Data
Wallace, Lorraine.
Mr. and Mrs. Sunday's suppers / Lorraine Wallace.
pages cm
ISBN 978-1-118-17529-3 (hardback); 978-0-544-18745-0 (ebk)
1. Cooking for two. 2. Dinners and dining.
I.Title. II. Title: Mister and missus Sunday's suppers.
TX714.W26186 2015
641.5′612—dc23
2014011682

Printed in the United States of America
DOC 10 9 8 7 6 5 4 3 2
4500525504

CONTENTS

ACKNOWLEDGMENTS

I am grateful to the many dedicated and talented people who helped make this book possible.

Thank you:

My husband Chris and our children—Peter, Megan, Catherine, Andrew, Sarah, and Remick—for the love and encouragement that they give me unconditionally.

Mom, for teaching me to always use organic ingredients, and how to cook.

My family, for both recipes and memories: Kappy Leonard, Pauline and Richard Bourgeois, Jennifer Wallace and our grandchildren William, Caroline, and James. And Miguel Calderon and granddaughters Sabine and Livia Calderon Wallace.

My friends: Ann Free, Josh Bowman, Ricky Lauren, Nancy Ellison, Nelson Sigelman, Josh Muss, Patty Warrender, and Liz Dubin for sharing their favorite supper recipes.

Chefs I admire: Chef Bill Smith of Crook's Corner restaurant, Frank Pellegrino of Rao's, Chef Billy Martin of Martin's Tavern, the Lobel family and Lobel's New York, Chef Luigi Diotaiuti of Al Tiramisu, Chef Ann Marie James of Wagshal's Deli, Molly Stevens, Christy and Libby Hughes of the Irish Inn, Myron Mixon, and José Andrés, for sharing their one-of-a-kind specialties.

Adam Mahr, Lou Shields, and Sue Bluford for wonderful tabletop and table-styling ideas.

My agent Michael Psaltis of the Culinary Entertainment Agency, who always helps me with the details and never lets me lose sight of the big picture.

Kelly Alexander, an award-winning food writer and editor, for her friendship and culinary expertise in tasting, testing, writing, and editing.

My editor, Justin Schwartz, for his vision and professionalism.

My publisher, Houghton Mifflin Harcourt, for believing in me and making my vision come true with all of their hard work.

Cover photographer Yassine El Mansouri for his keen eye for photography and for always making me look good.

Most of the recipes in this book are designed to serve 8. Feel free to scale them according to your needs. Cut them in half, quarter them, or double them as needed.

And send me your feedback at my website, www.mrssunday.com.

All my best wishes from my kitchen to yours!

Lauraine Wallace

COME TO SUPPER

"LORRAINE, ARE WE EATING TONIGHT?" That is the joking way my husband, Chris (aka Mr. Sunday), asks me when supper will be ready. Like so many families, I have to figure out how to put a meal on the table on a busy work night—and also for special larger family gatherings. It has to be reasonably quick and easy, but also I want it to be delicious. This is a hard balance to strike, and yet we all crave spending time together over a tasty and satisfying meal at the end of a hard day of work.

For many years, I balanced the schedules, after-school activities, and appointments for our blended family. And that is not to mention their likes and dislikes and dietary restrictions. And through this experience I believe it is important for everyone in a family to sit down together for supper. There are studies that show children learn to cope better with their anxieties when they share a meal with their parents and siblings. They have a chance to discuss the highs and lows of their days and to unwind together. Now, I realize that every supper cannot be a culinary hit, but I have always tried to make each evening meal special and I hope that in this book, *Mr. and Mrs. Sunday's Suppers*, you can find a guideline to help you get supper on the table.

Chris and I are empty-nesters now, but that does not make the task easier—actually, cooking for two is the same challenge. And the goal is still the same: to sit down for supper and share our experiences at the end of the day, whether we're by ourselves or some of our adult children drop in for a home-cooked meal. The most important thing I've learned is that with just a little effort and great ingredients, a satisfying supper isn't very difficult, and all of the recipes in this book are designed to help you do just that: Create great meals that aren't a struggle or a chore. I'm giving you a formula for success, from my kitchen to yours!

What is supper? While dinner and supper are often used interchangeably to mean the evening meal, most of the recipes in this book are for the kind of meal you probably only use one pot to prepare, whether you bake, braise, or sauté them. Most of the recipes in this book serve eight, and I encourage you to make the eight portions even if it's just two of you, as nothing makes a week easier than having leftovers. I also thought eight was a good number of servings because you can just split the recipe in half if you want it to yield less.

Last but not least is the Sunday Suppers chapter, which I hope will provide you with insight about the tradition of

the Sunday meal and some ideas to start your own. Here I give you whole supper suggestions, including delicious sides and desserts to make the meal complete.

I want to dispel the notion that supper has to mean a frazzled, harried experience for the home cook. And I do consider myself a home cook. I never dreamed of writing a cookbook. My first, *Mr. Sunday's Soups*, came about because I was looking for a way to get my family together for a quick Sunday lunch before we all headed our separate ways. And soup was the perfect solution. It worked so well for my family that I started sharing my recipes with friends. When I realized I had enough soups to fill a book, I had to put up with some doubts—even from my loving husband. But I pressed on. I call that the "Little Book That Could" and you helped make it a bestseller!

My second book, *Mr. Sunday's Saturday Night Chicken*, came about the very same way. When Chris took over as the anchor of *Fox News Sunday*, I asked him what he wanted to eat the night before his first show. The answer was chicken, because it is his comfort food, and for over ten years we've eaten chicken every Saturday night. As Chris likes to say, "Change is overrated."

This book is inspired by all of my family and friends, and the readers who enjoy my recipes. I hear a lot about how hard it is to make time to unplug and schedule a good supper in our busy world. I know exactly how that feels, and I know that with a collection of solid, tried-and-true, and yet delicious meals, it doesn't have to be.

So in this third book, *Mr. and Mrs. Sunday Suppers*, I share with you my most personal recipes to date, the ones I rely on as solutions to the supper dilemma. *Welcome to my kitchen.*

GETTING CHILDREN INVOLVED

The best way to make supper special is to get children involved in a dinnertime ritual. Start out by having them help set the table. Go to an art store and have them each select a small, inexpensive bud vase. Then they can take their vases and go to the yard and cut a flower to put on the table, or choose a bloom from a nearby nursery; get enough to last a few days. Another idea is to have them give ideas for supper theme nights, like Italian food night, Mexican food night, or even "favorite hat" night. (We have three grandchildren who wear matching pajamas to dinner each night—and they must match or tears abound and feelings are hurt.) A great way to have fun is to buy a roll of craft paper and tape a big piece down instead of a tablecloth or placemats, then let the kids have at it with crayons or colored pencils—and the grown-ups, too.

SETTING THE TABLE

When you are setting the table for your suppers, think like an artist! Here's how I do it: The first step is to consider the season and what kind of meal you are preparing. Once you decide on the meal, the next step is to consider colors, shapes, and sizes. You want complementary and contrasting colors on the table, from the food to the flatware. Here are my best tips:

Family members moving or downsizing? Ask to repurpose any linens, tureens, plates, planters' vases, and pots. The best part is that now they're "heirloom."

Take a large glass or pewter bowl and fill it with green or red apples, mini pumpkins and gourds, or even tricolored grapes and lemons.

If you have terra-cotta pots in the garden filled with fresh herbs like rosemary, basil, lavender, or thyme, repurpose them as natural centerpieces.

Mix and match plates from different settings for variety and whimsy.

For your appetizer or salad plate, use a small colored glass plate on top of a favorite larger dinner plate.

I like simple table linens in solids, lightly printed fabrics, or delicate paisley prints.

Instead of individual placemats, use a runner down the center of the table.

In lieu of a large floral centerpiece, take bud vases of different sizes and fill them with small flowers from your garden.

Unearth your cake stand and pile it with seasonal vegetables like eggplant, zucchini, and yellow squash in the summer.

Instead of dishing out individual bowls of soup in the kitchen, place a large soup tureen in the middle of the table and ladle out to each person at the table.

Invest in colored stemware to use as water glasses to brighten the table.

Make seasonal placeholders: For instance at Easter, dye your own eggs in various colors and use a metallic marker to write each person's name on it.

Bring the outside to the table: I often bring in dogwood and cherry blossom branches to decorate my table in early spring. In winter, I fill a large wooden bowl with acorns or pinecones and use it as a centerpiece.

NOTES ABOUT SALAD

In many recipes in this book, I recommend serving the supper with "A Simple Green Salad." The truth is that I could recommend that you serve all of the recipes in this book alongside a simple green salad. Salad is my favorite side dish, not least because I don't have to cook it! There is, however, both an art and science to making a good salad. A "simple green salad" doesn't mean the same thing to everyone, and some people may not have arrived at the perfect formula. So I'm going to offer up the best green salad in my repertoire for you right here.

Not all salads are green, of course. There are other really nice ways to serve healthful raw veggies besides ensconced in lettuce leaves. So I'm also offering you another of my favorite salads, and some other ideas for leafless salads, to help you get veggies on the table without having to cook anything at all.

A SIMPLE GREEN SALAD

The most important part of the art of making a superb salad is choosing the freshest ingredients, especially vegetables and fruits that are ripe during the season. They will taste better and provide your family with better nutrition, and the added bonus is they are budget friendly. Here I offer you a basic recipe for a fresh green salad that you can enhance or adapt to what you have in your pantry.

Serves 8

- ⅓ cup extra-virgin olive oil
- 1 large shallot, minced (about 1½ tablespoons)
- ¼ cup champagne vinegar or red wine vinegar
  Coarse salt and freshly ground pepper
- 2 large heads butter lettuce, leaves separated
- 2 cups loosely packed fresh flat-leaf parsley leaves
- 1 cup loosely packed fresh cilantro leaves, fresh chervil sprigs, or chopped tender green onion, or a combination

1. In the bottom of a large salad bowl, combine the oil with the shallot. Add the vinegar and season with salt and pepper, and whisk. Top with the lettuce, parsley, and the other herbs of your choice.

2. You can cover the salad bowl with a damp paper towel and refrigerate until ready to serve for up to 3 hours.

3. When ready to serve, toss well and mound the salad on individual serving plates.

TIP: How easy is it to make croutons? As easy as taking cubes of leftover toast, cornbread, or even polenta, brushing them with a little oil, seasoning with salt and pepper, and toasting them at 325°F for 10 minutes or until crisp. You'll never have to buy them in the store again.

TIP: You can jazz up this salad by adding grated hard cheese, like Parmesan, or crumbled soft cheese, like goat cheese or mozzarella balls. And you can always add crunch to a salad by tossing in toasted almonds, pine nuts, cashews, or walnuts.

CELERY HEART SALAD

So many of us buy celery for a stalk or two and then forget about the rest. This recipe celebrates celery and its bright, fresh, crisp nature. The salad is a perfect side for a hearty, rich stew.

Serves 8

- ¼ cup plain Greek yogurt
  Grated zest from 1 large lemon (about 2 teaspoons)
- ¼ cup lemon juice
- ¼ cup extra-virgin olive oil
- 2 medium shallots, finely minced (about 2 tablespoons)
- 1 teaspoon celery seed
  Coarse salt and freshly ground pepper
- ¾ cup pine nuts
- 2 heads celery hearts, tender leaves included, sliced thinly on an angle (about 6 cups)
- ½ cup grated Parmesan cheese
- 1 cup loosely packed fresh flat-leaf parsley leaves

1. Several hours prior to serving the salad, in a medium bowl whisk together the yogurt, lemon zest, lemon juice, oil, shallots, and celery seed. Season with salt and pepper and set aside.

2. In a small skillet, toast the pine nuts over medium-low heat, shaking the skillet occasionally, until golden, about 4 minutes. Transfer the pine nuts to a small bowl and set aside.

3. In a large nonreactive bowl, combine the celery slices with the dressing and stir to combine well. Cover and refrigerate up to 3 hours to allow the celery to absorb the flavors and crisp.

4. When ready to serve, arrange the celery on a long, flat platter. Sprinkle the cheese, parsley, and pine nuts over the celery.

IDEAS FOR OTHER LEAFLESS SALADS:

Shaved salads are quick to make and best left to prepare minutes before you plan to serve them.

SHRED IT: Shredded carrots, zucchini, cucumbers, squash, cabbage: All of these can be simply dressed with a little bit of oil, a squeeze or two of fresh lemon, salt, and pepper, and then tossed together—and you can always add in a bit of whatever fresh herb you have on hand.

Stocking the Seasonal Pantry, Fridge, and Freezer

The key to building a pantry, refrigerator, and freezer is in selecting and rotating ingredients around the seasons. This will help with your menu planning and weekly marketing and prove to be friendly to your wallet. With these ingredients at your fingertips, you will see that it is just as fast and easy to whip up your own creative fresh meals at home. If you have the basics listed below and rotate your proteins and fresh vegetables according to what is fresh and local at your market, you will always have exactly the things you need for a simple seasonal supper. This list is a guideline and includes more than you'll need, but remember two things: I only need to buy small quantities of most of these items, since I replace my pantry every season; and some of the items are perennials and worth an investment.

In the Pantry

Anchovy paste

Barley

Broths: organic beef, chicken, seafood, vegetable

Canned black beans, chickpeas, cannellini beans, kidney beans

Canned tomatoes: diced, crushed, and whole, plus sauce and paste

Coconut milk

Couscous: regular, pearl

Dates

Dried pastas: orzo, tagliatelle, penne, macaroni, fettuccine, linguine, ditalini

Dried split peas, white beans, black beans, lentils

Garlic paste

Grits, polenta, or both: whole, stone-ground

Nuts: pine nuts, walnuts, pecan halves, almonds

Panko bread crumbs

Plain or Italian dried bread crumbs

Prunes

Quinoa

Raisins: golden, brown

Rice: brown, white

Tuna, water-packed

Water chestnuts

Baking

Baking powder

Baking soda

Chocolate bricks: dark (70% semisweet), white

Chocolate morsels: semisweet, milk, white, butterscotch

Cocoa powder

Coconut: flaked, shredded

Cornmeal

Cornstarch

Extracts: lemon, vanilla

Flour: all-purpose, rice, whole wheat

Sugar: brown, granulated, superfine, confectioner's

Fruits and Vegetables

Garlic

Leeks

Lemons

Limes

Onions: red, sweet, white

Oranges

Potatoes: sweet, white

Scallions

Squash

Spice Drawer

Basil

Bay leaves

Cayenne pepper

Coarse sea salt

Coriander

Cream of tartar

Crushed red pepper flakes

Cumin

Dry mustard

Garlic salt and powder

Ground cinnamon

Herbes de Provence

Italian seasoning

Nutmeg

Old Bay Seasoning

Parsley flakes

Peppercorns: black, tricolored, white

Rosemary

Saffron threads

Sage

Thyme

Turmeric

In the Fridge

Agave syrup

Honey: orange blossom

Hot sauce: sriracha, red and green Tabasco

Maple syrup

Mustard: Dijon, honey, country

Pickles: dill, jalapeño, relish, pepper rings

Soy sauce

Tahini

Teriyaki sauce

Worcestershire sauce

Vinegars and Oils

Oils: canola, olive, grape, sesame, corn, nonstick cooking spray

Vinegars: white wine, red wine, balsamic, champagne, apple cider

In the Freezer

Berries

Corn

Kale

Lima beans

Mixed vegetables

Peas

Spinach

SUPPER SOUPS AND STEWS

It all began with soup. My career as a cookbook author, that is. But even before that, soup has always been the foundation of our family time. "Soup was Lorraine's way to bring us together. And we all loved it," Chris wrote in the foreword to *Mr. Sunday's Soups*. And he's right. Making soup was the way I kept my family at the table with one another; it bound us, it helped us stay in each other's lives. So after a few years of gathering my clan for an early Sunday lunch of homemade soup I had amassed what I thought was a terrific collection of tried-and-true soup winners, and I shared many of them with you in my first cookbook.

I was amazed and gratified by how well that book was received and by how many friends old and new have come forward to tell me about their favorite soups. (If I'm going to be remembered for just one thing, "the soup lady" is really not so bad.)

As a result my soup recipe collection grew even bigger. I've also found that soups work well for suppers. So it seems like there's no better place to start this book than with some quick, easy, delicious, and good-for-you soup recipes.

You can double any of these recipes, make a big batch, and then enjoy it during the hectic weeknights. All you need to do is add a nice green salad, and maybe a pan or two of savory muffins, popovers, or just some warm and crusty bread and, *presto*, you have supper on the table. Soup travels well for potluck and buffet dinners with friends, too.

When the cooler weather hits, preparing the slower-cooking stews in this chapter offers an especially satisfying way to while away a winter afternoon. These hearty mixtures take a little longer to cook, but the mouthwatering smells in your kitchen will entice everyone in your family to the table. Stews are good to freeze, too, so you can spend more time during the holidays and football season celebrating with your family.

BEEF STEW WITH WINTER ROOT VEGETABLES

From the kitchen of Joshua Bowman

This beef stew cooks long enough to reduce so you do not need to make a roux to thicken it. And the longer it cooks, the better it tastes—plus your house will smell great from the aroma. Josh says to do "the spoon test": Dip a spoon into the stew and if the liquid coats the backside of the spoon, you know it is just the right consistency.

Serves 8

- 1½ cups port wine or any sweet red wine or beef broth if you're avoiding alcohol
- 2 ounces dried mushrooms, porcini or morel or a combination (about ½ cup)
- 1 cup extra-virgin olive oil
- 4 pounds boneless beef chuck roast, cut into 1-inch pieces
-    Coarse salt and freshly ground pepper
- 6 large garlic cloves
- 3 medium celery stalks, finely chopped (about 1½ cups)
- 2 large yellow onions, coarsely chopped (about 2¼ cups)
- 3 large carrots, peeled and cut into 1-inch pieces (about 2 cups)
- 3 cups beef broth, homemade or store-bought
- 2 cups dry red wine or beef broth if you're avoiding alcohol
- 3 tablespoons tomato paste
- 4 sprigs fresh thyme plus 2 teaspoons finely chopped fresh thyme
- 2 tablespoons dried sage
- 1 tablespoon fresh rosemary leaves or 1 teaspoon dried
- 4 bay leaves
- 3 medium parsnips or turnips or a combination of the two, peeled and cut into 1-inch pieces (about 2 cups)
- 1 tablespoon Worcestershire sauce
- 1 pound egg noodles, cooked and buttered (optional), for serving
- 2 tablespoons coarsely grated fresh horseradish (optional), for serving

1. In a small bowl, combine the port with the dried mushrooms and let soak for 20 minutes to reconstitute. After 20 minutes, strain the mushrooms through a fine mesh strainer, reserving both the mushrooms and the soaking liquid separately.

2. In a Dutch oven or large, heavy stockpot, heat 1 tablespoon of the oil over medium-high heat. Working in batches, add the beef, season it generously with salt and pepper, and cook until lightly browned on all sides, turning frequently, 6 to 8 minutes total for each batch. Transfer the browned meat to a large bowl and cover loosely with foil to rest until all of the meat is finished cooking.

3. Return all of the browned meat to the pot and add half of the garlic along with the celery, onions, and carrots. Pour in the beef broth and dry red wine. Add the mushroom liquid along with the remaining oil, the tomato paste, thyme, sage, rosemary, and bay leaves. Cover, bring the mixture to a boil over medium-high heat (about 12 minutes), uncover, reduce the heat to medium-low, and cook at a simmer for 1½ hours. Add the soaked mushrooms and the remaining garlic, stir well to combine, and continue to simmer for another hour. Add the parsnips and Worcestershire sauce and continue to cook until the stew is thickened, about 30 minutes longer (about 3 hours total cooking time). Discard the bay leaves and thyme sprigs.

4. Serve in warmed large rimmed bowls with the egg noodles and grated horseradish on the side, if you like.

TIP
Right before you serve the stew, you can stir in a teaspoon of dried mustard; it really enhances the flavor and thickens the stew.

BRUNSWICK STEW

From the kitchen of Billy Martin at Martin's Tavern in Washington, D.C.

Martin's Tavern, which has been an institution in D.C. since it opened in 1933, is a great standby for Mr. and Mrs. Sunday's date nights, and we love their Brunswick Stew. Every town named Brunswick from Canada to the Carolinas has tried to claim this stew as its own. However, Brunswick County in Virginia is where we place our bet, especially since the dish has been a staple at tobacco curings and public gatherings since the state began. Historians argue about what precisely went into the original pot, and what should go in it now. The story goes that a hunting party in Brunswick County, well provisioned with tomatoes, onions, cabbage, butter beans, red pepper, bacon, salt, and corn, left one man behind to mind the commissary and to have dinner ready at day's end. Disgruntled, he shot a squirrel, the only thing he could find within range of the camp, and threw it into the pot along with the vegetables. When it was served, everybody agreed that the squirrel was what made the new stew just right. However, chicken is substituted now. "It is a rule in some tidewater homes never to eat Brunswick Stew the same day it is made, because its flavor improves if it is left to stand overnight and reheated the next day," owner Billy Martin says. "This is our rule!" (He also recommends that you eat it with some cornbread on the side.)

Serves 8

- One 6-pound stewing hen or two 3-pound broiler-fryer chickens
- 3 medium onions, diced (about 4 cups)
- 3 medium celery stalks, diced (about 1½ cups)
- 3 medium carrots, peeled and diced (about 1 cup)
- 2 bay leaves
- 1 tablespoon coarse salt, plus more to taste
- 1 teaspoon freshly ground pepper, plus more to taste
- 2½ quarts (10 cups) water, or more as needed
- 3 medium potatoes, peeled and diced (about 3 cups)
- One 28-ounce can whole plum tomatoes, juices drained
- One 16-ounce bag frozen okra, thawed
- One 16-ounce bag frozen corn, thawed
- One 14-ounce bag frozen lima beans, thawed
- 1 tablespoon sugar

1. In a large, heavy stockpot, combine the chicken with the onions, celery, carrots, bay leaves, salt, and pepper. Cover with at least 2 ½ cups of water. Bring to a boil over high heat. Reduce the heat to medium and cook until the chicken falls from the bone, about 1½ hours. Remove the chicken from the broth to cool on a cutting board. When cool enough to handle, discard the skin and use your fingers to pull the meat from the bones. Set aside the shredded chicken meat.

2. Add the potatoes, tomatoes, okra, corn, and lima beans to the broth. Simmer, uncovered, stirring occasionally to prevent scorching and using the back of a wooden spoon to break up some of the whole tomatoes, until the potatoes are tender, about 25 minutes. Stir in the sugar. Add the chicken back to the stew and heat until warmed through, 5 to 10 minutes. Taste and adjust the seasoning with additional salt and pepper, if needed, and discard the bay leaves. Serve immediately, piping hot.

BUFFALO TURKEY CHILI

This recipe is back by popular demand from my soup cookbook! More people inquire—call me, text me, and email me—about this recipe than any other. It's easy, you can make it ahead of time, it's a beautiful color, and it doesn't even contain the controversial ingredient in some chilis—beans.

Serves 8

- 3 tablespoons vegetable oil
- 4 pounds ground turkey
- Coarse salt and freshly ground pepper
- 5 tablespoons unsalted butter
- 1¼ cups Crystal Hot Sauce or your own personal favorite
- Two 28-ounce cans diced tomatoes, with their juices
- 1 quart (4 cups) chicken stock, homemade or store-bought
- 8 garlic cloves, chopped
- One 7-ounce can diced green chiles, with their juices
- ⅓ cup tomato paste
- 1½ tablespoons crushed red pepper flakes
- 3 to 4 cups crumbled blue cheese or grated mild cheddar or pepper Jack cheese, for topping

1. Place a large, heavy stockpot or Dutch oven over medium heat and add 1½ tablespoons of the oil. Add half of the turkey, season with salt and pepper, and cook, stirring and breaking up the meat, until browned. Transfer to a bowl with a slotted spoon. Add the remaining 1½ tablespoons oil to the pot and repeat the process with the remaining turkey. Return the first batch of turkey and any accumulated juices to the pot.

2. In a small saucepan over medium heat, melt the butter. Stir in the hot sauce. Add the hot sauce mixture to the turkey, along with the tomatoes and their juices, stock, and garlic. Bring the mixture to a boil over high heat, then reduce the heat to low and simmer gently until reduced by a third, about 1½ hours.

3. Stir in the green chiles and their juices, tomato paste, and red pepper flakes, and simmer to cook off the raw flavor of the tomato paste, about 15 minutes more.

4. Ladle into shallow bowls and scatter with the cheese of your choice. Serve immediately.

CHICKEN SOUP WITH FENNEL AND APPLES

This seasonal soup recipe incorporates sweet apples and savory fennel, lending it a special warmth and richness for a crisp fall day.

Serves 8

- 2½ to 3 pounds boneless skinless chicken breasts
- 1 quart (4 cups) water
- 12 ounces chicken apple sausage
- 2 tablespoons extra-virgin olive oil
- 3 medium onions, sliced into ½-inch slices (about 3 cups)
- 3 medium carrots, peeled and coarsely chopped (about 1 cup)
- 2 to 3 medium celery stalks, coarsely chopped (about 1 cup)
- 6 garlic cloves, minced
- 2 teaspoons ground cumin
- 2 teaspoons dried thyme
- 3 quarts (12 cups) chicken broth, homemade or store-bought
- 4 medium Granny Smith apples, peeled, cored, and sliced into ¼-inch-thick matchsticks (about 4 cups)
- 1 small head green cabbage, shredded (about 3 cups)
- 2 tablespoons apple cider vinegar
- 1 tablespoon dried fennel
- ½ teaspoon coarse salt
- ½ teaspoon freshly ground pepper

1. Rinse the chicken with cold water and pat dry with paper towels. Place a large skillet with a tight-fitting lid over medium-high heat. Add the water and the chicken breasts. Bring to a simmer, then immediately remove the skillet from the heat. Cover and let stand until the chicken is tender, about 15 minutes. Transfer the chicken breasts to a plate and let cool.

2. Place the sausages in a large lightly greased skillet over medium-high heat and cook until golden brown on all sides, about 3 minutes. Remove the sausages from the pan onto a paper towel–lined plate and set aside to cool. When cool enough to handle, slice into ½-inch-thick rounds.

3. Heat the oil in a large, heavy stockpot or Dutch oven over medium heat. Add the onion, carrot, celery, and garlic, and cook until the vegetables are softened, 10 to 12 minutes. Add the sliced sausage and cook for 2 minutes more. Add the cumin and thyme and, stirring constantly, cook for 1 minute more.

4. Add the broth to the pot and bring to a boil. Cover the pot, reduce the heat to low, and allow the soup to remain at a gentle simmer for 20 minutes.

5. Meanwhile, using your hands, shred the poached chicken into thin pieces.

6. Increase the heat to medium-high, add the chicken, apples, cabbage, vinegar, fennel, salt, and pepper, and cook until the meat is heated through and the apples, cabbage, and fennel have softened, about 10 minutes. Serve immediately, in warmed bowls, if you like.

COD BOUILLABAISSE

This one-pot meal has everything that makes fresh cod shine: a full-flavored broth, spicy chorizo, and tender potatoes and leeks. Be sure to use smoked paprika in the aioli—it's not hard to find on most spice racks in good markets these days, and it adds a fiery flavor.

Serves 8

- 1 cup mayonnaise
- ½ cup extra-virgin olive oil
- 1 teaspoon smoked paprika
- 8 garlic cloves, minced
- 12 ounces chorizo sausage, cut into ¼-inch dice
- 4 medium leeks, white and tender green parts only, halved lengthwise and sliced into very thin strips (about 2 cups)
- 2 pounds Yukon gold potatoes, scrubbed and cut into a ¾-inch dice
- One 28-ounce can diced tomatoes, with their juices
- 2 cups dry white wine
- Coarse salt and freshly ground pepper
- 4 skinless cod loins, cut into 8 fillets (about 3 pounds)
- ½ cup finely chopped fresh flat-leaf parsley (optional), for serving

1. In a medium bowl, whisk together the mayonnaise, 1 tablespoon of the oil, the paprika, and 1 teaspoon of the garlic in a bowl until thoroughly combined. Cover with plastic wrap and refrigerate until ready to serve.

2. In a large Dutch oven, heat 1 tablespoon of the oil over medium-high heat. Add the chorizo and cook until lightly browned, about 3 minutes. Using a slotted spoon, transfer the chorizo to a plate, leaving the fat in the pot.

3. Add the leeks and cook, stirring, until the leeks soften, about 5 minutes. Add the remaining garlic and cook until just fragrant, about 30 seconds. Add the potatoes, tomatoes with their juices, and wine to the pot and cook, partially covered, until the potatoes become soft, 12 to 15 minutes.

4. Stir in the chorizo and season the broth with salt and pepper to taste. Let the mixture come to a low simmer, then turn down the heat.

5. Meanwhile, wash the cod and, using a paper towel, pat the fillets dry. Season the pieces with salt and pepper. Nestle the fish fillets on top of the broth and simmer, covered, until the fish is cooked through, 6 to 8 minutes.

6. Serve the soup in warmed large wide-rimmed bowls topped with a dollop of the prepared aioli and, if you like, a sprinkling of parsley.

CHICKEN AND DUMPLINGS

This is my winter substitute recipe instead of roasting a chicken—and it's one of the dishes Chris likes on a Saturday night prior to doing his show. When you add the herb dumplings this becomes a hearty meal.

Serves 8

FOR THE SOUP

- 1½ quarts (6 cups) chicken broth, homemade or store-bought
- 3 pounds whole chicken legs, including thighs and drumsticks (about 4 to 5 legs)
- 2 cups water
- 2 sprigs fresh thyme or 1½ teaspoons dried
- 2 sprigs fresh flat-leaf parsley o r 1½ teaspoons dried
- 1 bay leaf
- 2 tablespoons extra-virgin olive oil
- 3 medium celery stalks, finely diced (about 1½ cups)
- 3 medium carrots, peeled and finely diced (about 1 cup)
- 1 small onion, finely chopped (about ⅔ cup)
- 2 garlic cloves, thinly sliced
- ¾ teaspoon coarse salt
- Freshly ground pepper

FOR THE DUMPLINGS

- 1¼ cups all-purpose flour
- 2 teaspoons baking powder
- 1½ teaspoons finely chopped fresh dill
- ¼ teaspoon coarse salt
- Freshly ground pepper
- 2 tablespoons unsalted butter, cut into 4 pieces
- ½ cup buttermilk
- 1 large egg, lightly beaten

1. **TO MAKE THE SOUP:** In a large saucepan, combine the broth, chicken, water, thyme, parsley, and bay leaf. Place over medium-high heat and bring the mixture to a boil. Reduce the heat to low and simmer very gently until the chicken is firm and cooked through to the center, 15 to 18 minutes. Skim the foam off the top with a large, flat spoon. Remove the pan from the heat and let cool for 5 to 10 minutes.

2. Lift the chicken from the broth and, when cool enough to handle, remove the meat from the bones and chop into bite-size pieces. Set aside. Strain the broth through a fine-mesh sieve into a large bowl and discard the herb sprigs and bay leaf.

3. Place a large, heavy stockpot or Dutch oven over medium-low heat and add the oil. Add the celery, carrots, and onion, and cook, stirring, until the vegetables are softened, about 8 minutes. Add the garlic and cook, stirring, for 1 minute more.

4. Add the reserved broth, the salt, and pepper to taste. Return the chopped chicken to the soup. Cover and keep warm over very low heat while you make the dumpling mixture.

5. **TO MAKE THE DUMPLINGS:** In a large bowl, whisk together the flour, baking powder, dill, salt, and a little pepper. Work the butter into the mixture with a pastry cutter or your fingertips until it is the consistency of coarse breadcrumbs. In a small bowl, whisk the buttermilk and egg briefly, then, using a fork, blend the buttermilk mixture into the dry ingredients to form a thick and clumpy batter.

6. Bring the soup to a very gentle simmer. Working quickly, use 2 spoons to form 16 dumplings, each about 2 teaspoons in size, and drop them into the broth. Immediately cover the pot and cook at a very gentle simmer until the dumplings are firm, 7 to 10 minutes (do not let the soup boil). Ladle into warmed bowls and serve, distributing the dumplings, chicken, and vegetables evenly.

POLLO AL CHILINDRÓN

From the kitchen of José Andrés

The award-winning and wildly talented Spanish-born chef José Andrés has made Washington, D.C., his home for years, and we love visiting his restaurants—the food is always authentic and delicious. José explains: "Chilindrón (chicken with peppers, tomatoes, onions, and Spanish ham) is a wonderful vegetable stew that comes from Aragon, where they grow astonishing vegetables in the fertile land near the Ebro River."

Serves 8

- ¾ cup extra-virgin olive oil, preferably Spanish
- 8 chicken legs, thighs and drumsticks, separated (about 2 to 2 ½ pounds)
- Coarse salt
- 4 large Spanish onions, diced (about 8 cups)
- 1 large green bell pepper, diced (about 2 cups)
- 1 large red bell pepper, diced (about 2 cups)
- 6 to 8 garlic cloves, minced (about ¼ cup)
- 2 cups dry white wine
- 12 ounces jamón serrano (Spanish cured ham), thinly sliced and diced (about 2 cups)
- 4 cups tomato sauce
- 1 quart (4 cups) water
- 1 teaspoon sweet pimentón (Spanish smoked paprika)
- 2 sprigs fresh rosemary
- 2 bay leaves

1. Heat ¼ cup of the oil in a large, heavy stockpot over medium-high heat. Season the chicken pieces with salt, then, working in batches, brown them on all sides. Transfer the chicken to a platter and set aside.

2. Add the remaining ½ cup oil to the same pot. Once the oil is hot, add the onions and bell peppers. Reduce the heat to medium and cook slowly until the onions are dark golden brown, about 30 minutes. Add 1 tablespoon of water if the onions start to burn. Add the garlic and cook for 5 more minutes. Then add the wine and cook until it evaporates, 4 to 5 minutes.

3. Add the jamón and the browned chicken pieces, as well as any juices that have collected, and cook for 5 more minutes. Stir in the tomato sauce, water, pimentón, rosemary, and bay leaves and simmer over low heat until the meat starts to fall off the bone, about 1 hour. Discard the rosemary sprig and bay leaves. Season to taste with salt before serving.

GUMBO BIG EASY

From the kitchen of Kelly Alexander

My friend and collaborator Kelly Alexander, who worked on the staff of several major food magazines, loves gumbo—but she has two small kids and few opportunities during the week for time-consuming recipes. So she devised this version, which she can make in just over an hour, and saves it for the weekends. For best results, wait to buy the shrimp until the day, or at most the day before, you plan to serve this.

Serves 8

⅓ cup vegetable oil

½ pound andouille or other spicy smoked sausage, casing removed, halved lengthwise and cut crosswise into ¼-inch slices

2 pounds boneless chicken thighs (about 12 to 16 pieces)

½ cup all-purpose flour

2 medium onions, finely chopped (about 1¼ cups)

2 medium celery stalks with leaves, finely chopped (about 1 cup)

1 medium red bell pepper, finely chopped (about ½ cup)

1 medium green bell pepper, finely chopped (about ½ cup)

3 garlic cloves, minced

1½ quarts (6 cups) chicken stock, homemade or store-bought

One 28-ounce can plum tomatoes, with their juices, coarsely chopped (about 3½ cups)

1½ teaspoons dried thyme

2 teaspoons coarse salt

1 bay leaf

¼ teaspoon cayenne pepper

3 cups water

1½ cups long-grain white rice

¼ cup chopped fresh or thawed frozen okra

1 pound medium to large shrimp, peeled and deveined (16 to 20 count)

2 scallions, including green tops, minced (about ¼ cup)

¼ cup coarsely chopped fresh flat-leaf parsley

½ teaspoon Tabasco or other favorite hot sauce

¼ teaspoon freshly ground pepper

1. In a large, heavy stockpot, heat the oil over medium-high heat. Add the andouille. Cook until the sausage is browned, about 4 minutes. With a slotted spoon, remove the sausage. Add half of the chicken thighs to the pot. Brown on both sides, about 8 minutes in all. Remove and set aside. Repeat with the remaining chicken.

2. Reduce the heat to medium and let the fat cool slightly. Stir in the flour to make a roux. If the sausage hasn't rendered enough fat, the mixture may be crumbly; add a little oil if needed. Cook, stirring frequently, until the roux turns brown. Stir the mixture constantly until dark brown, about 10 minutes.

3. Add the onions, celery, bell peppers, and garlic, and cook, stirring, for 1 minute. Stir in the stock, tomatoes with their juices, thyme, 1½ teaspoons of the salt, the bay leaf, and cayenne. Cut the chicken thighs into bite-size pieces and add them to the pot. Cook, partially covered, stirring occasionally, until the vegetables are very tender, about 40 minutes. (The soup may be made ahead up to this point a day or two in advance and stored, covered, in the refrigerator.)

4. Meanwhile, bring the water to a boil with the remaining ½ teaspoon salt. Add the rice. Reduce the heat, cover, and simmer until the rice is tender and all the water is absorbed, 20 to 25 minutes.

5. Add the cooked sausage and okra to the soup and cook, covered, for 10 minutes. Add the shrimp and cook just until the shrimp are done, 2 to 3 minutes more. Discard the bay leaf. Stir in the scallions, 2 tablespoons of the parsley, the Tabasco, and the pepper.

6. Stir the remaining 2 tablespoons parsley into the rice. Pack ⅓ cup of the rice into a measuring cup or small ramekin. Unmold in the center of a large soup plate and repeat with the remaining rice. Ladle the gumbo around the rice.

Peruvian Chicken Soup (Aguadito de Pollo)

Our son Remick loves this soup! It's a traditional Peruvian dish that contains large pieces of chicken and potatoes cooked with peas, corn, and red pepper. It's meant to be very green, enriched using lots of cilantro (and Remick always asks me to make the broth even greener than that). I often make a double batch so I can send him home with individual storage containers to pack for his lunch to save time and money.

Serves 8

- 4 bone-in, skin-on chicken thighs (about 1½ pounds)
- 4 bone-in, skin-on chicken drumsticks (about 1½ pounds)
- Coarse salt and freshly ground pepper
- ½ cup extra-virgin olive oil
- 2 cups chopped fresh cilantro
- 3½ quarts (14 cups) chicken broth, homemade or store-bought
- 2 large garlic cloves
- 1 tablespoon minced seeded serrano chile pepper
- 1 medium onion, finely chopped (about ⅔ cup)
- 1 large red bell pepper, finely chopped (about ½ cup)
- 2 teaspoons ground cumin
- 1 cup uncooked, rinsed, and drained long-grain white rice
- 8 small Yukon gold potatoes, peeled
- 1 cup frozen peas, thawed
- 1 cup frozen corn, thawed
- 8 lime wedges (optional), for serving

1. Wash the chicken pieces and pat dry thoroughly with paper towels. Season each piece with salt and pepper. In a large, heavy stockpot, heat half of the oil over medium-high heat. Add the chicken pieces, skin-side down, and cook until browned, about 5 minutes, then flip over and brown on the other side. Remove the chicken from the pot and set aside on a platter to rest. Wipe out the pot with a paper towel and set aside.

2. In a blender, combine the cilantro, ½ cup of the broth, the garlic, and chili pepper. Blend until the mixture is thoroughly combined; it will be somewhat chunky and vividly green. Set aside.

3. Place the same large, heavy soup pot over medium-high heat and add the remaining oil. Add the onion and cook, stirring occasionally, until it is translucent, about 5 minutes. Add the bell pepper and cumin and cook until the pepper has softened, 1 to 2 minutes more. Add the rice and the cilantro mixture to the pot, stirring to completely coat the rice and vegetables. Gently add the chicken back into the pot. Pour in the remaining broth. Add the potatoes to the broth. Reduce the heat and simmer until the rice is fully cooked and the potatoes are soft, 20 to 25 minutes. Keep the soup warm over low heat until you are ready to serve it.

4. About 3 minutes before you are ready to serve, stir in the peas and corn and allow them to heat through. Season the soup to taste with salt and pepper. Serve in warmed bowls with the lime wedges on the side, if you like.

ITALIAN WEDDING SOUP

Tiny pork meatballs, chickpeas, earthy spinach, and naturally salty Parmesan combine for a marvelously filling soup, perfect for supper. Never throw away the rind of a wedge of Parmesan cheese! Save it in a baggie in the freezer and then add it to almost any soup to provide a little extra richness and tangy flavor.

Serves 8

- 2 tablespoons extra-virgin olive oil
- 2 large yellow onions, finely chopped (about 4 cups)
- 4 large carrots, peeled and finely diced (about 2 cups)
- 4 large celery stalks, finely diced (about 2 cups)
- 6 garlic cloves, minced (about ¼ cup)
- Coarse salt and freshly ground pepper
- 4 quarts (4 cups) chicken stock, homemade or store-bought
- 1½ pounds ground pork
- 1½ pounds Italian sausage
- 1 cup plain dried bread crumbs
- 1 cup grated Parmesan cheese
- 2 teaspoons dried Italian seasoning
- ¼ teaspoon crushed red pepper flakes
- 4 cups loosely packed baby spinach
- Three 15-ounce cans chickpeas, rinsed and drained
- 1 cup orzo, cooked al dente according to package directions
- Leaves fresh basil, torn (optional), for garnish

1. Heat the oil in a large, heavy stockpot over medium-high heat. Add the onions and cook, stirring, until softened and translucent but not yet brown, 4 to 6 minutes. Add the carrots, celery, and garlic, and season with salt and pepper; stir to combine and cook, stirring, about 5 minutes longer. Stir in the stock and turn the heat down and keep the soup on a low simmer.

2. In a large bowl, combine the pork, sausage, bread crumbs, cheese, Italian seasoning, and red pepper flakes. Season the mixture generously with salt and pepper. With your hands, knead the mixture gently to combine, taking care not to overmix. Using a two-teaspoon measuring spoon, form small meatballs about 1 inch in diameter.

3. Drop the balls into the simmering soup, and raise the heat to medium. Simmer the soup, partly covered, until the meatballs are cooked through, 25 to 30 minutes.

4. Add the spinach, chickpeas, and orzo and simmer, uncovered, for 20 minutes more.

5. Stir in the basil and cook until just wilted, if desired. Serve immediately in warmed large wide-rimmed bowls, if you like.

Vegetable Soup from the Summer Garden

This summer soup features luscious fresh tomatoes, tender squash, and sweet corn, ingredients that are abundant at our local markets and colorful roadside produce stands. Truly, this soup is meant to celebrate what's growing in our summer gardens, so skip it if you only have frozen veggies—and then, when in-season vegetables are available, make a double batch, freeze it, and on a cold winter day heat it up for a little reminder of summer when you need it most.

Serves 8

- 2 tablespoons extra-virgin olive oil
- 1 medium onion, diced (about ⅔ cup)
- 1 large leek, white and tender green parts only, cut in half and then thinly sliced lengthwise into thin strips (about 2 cups)
- 2 garlic cloves, finely minced
- 4 medium carrots, peeled and diced (about 1½ cups)
- 1 large celery stalk, diced (about ½ cup)
- 8 cups water
- 1 large rind Parmesan cheese (optional)
  Coarse salt
- One 28-ounce can diced tomatoes, with their juices, or 5 medium tomatoes, seeded and finely diced
- ¼ pound fresh green beans, trimmed and cut into ¼-inch pieces (about 2 cups)
- One 15-ounce can chickpeas, rinsed and drained
- 1 cup fresh corn kernels (about 2 ears corn)
- 1 medium zucchini, diced (about ⅔ cup)
- 1 medium yellow squash, diced (about ⅔ cup)
- ½ cup favorite small pasta, such as ditalini or macaroni
  Prepared pesto (optional), for serving

1. Heat the oil in a large, heavy stockpot or Dutch oven over medium-high heat. Add the onion and cook until golden and soft, 8 to 10 minutes. Add the leek and cook until softened, 3 to 4 minutes more. Add the garlic and cook until fragrant, about 1 minute longer. Add the carrots, celery, water, Parmesan rind, if using, and salt to taste; bring to a boil. Reduce the heat to low, and simmer, partially covered, for 10 minutes.

2. Add the tomatoes, green beans, chickpeas, corn, zucchini, and squash, increase the heat to medium-high, and bring back to a boil. Then reduce the heat to low and simmer, partially covered, until the vegetables are tender, about 30 minutes more. Taste and adjust the seasoning with additional salt, if needed. Let the soup continue to gently simmer while you cook the pasta according to package directions.

3. When ready to serve, ladle soup into warmed wide-rimmed bowls, add the pasta and stir to combine, and top each bowl with 1 tablespoon of pesto, if using.

Salmon Chowder with Pastry Crust

I like to use a puff pastry crust to dress up this chowder for a spring supper. I bake eight disks of puff pastry and place one on top of each bowl just prior to serving. If you have them, the classic French onion soup bowls with the little handles on either side of the bowl work well for the presentation. I prefer Dufour puff pastry dough, which is easy to find in the freezer section of most grocery stores.

Serves 8

- 4 ounces thick-sliced bacon, cut into ¼-inch dice
- 1 medium yellow onion, finely chopped (about ⅔ cup)
- 1½ pounds celery root, peeled and cut into ¼-inch dice (about 2 medium celery roots)
- 3 cups seafood broth or three 8-ounce bottles clam juice
- 3 cups water
- ½ pound tiny new potatoes, scrubbed and halved
- 2 pounds skinless salmon fillets (preferably wild-caught), cut into 1-inch chunks
- 1½ cups heavy cream
- 1 sheet frozen puff pastry, thawed
- 3 tablespoons unsalted butter, softened
- 3 tablespoons all-purpose flour
- 3 tablespoons finely chopped fresh dill
- 2 tablespoons finely chopped fresh flat-leaf parsley
- 1 teaspoon finely grated lemon zest
- 2 tablespoons lemon juice
- ¼ teaspoon coarse salt
- ¼ teaspoon freshly ground pepper
- 1 large egg, beaten with a teaspoon of water and a pinch of coarse salt

1. In a large skillet, cook the bacon over low heat until crisp; transfer to a paper towel–lined plate and pour off all but 2 tablespoons of the fat from the skillet.

2. Add the onion to the skillet and cook, stirring, until softened, about 3 minutes. Add the celery root, cover the skillet, and cook, stirring occasionally, until tender, about 15 minutes. Set the skillet aside.

3. In a large, heavy saucepan, combine the broth and water. Bring to a boil and add the potatoes. Simmer until the potatoes are tender, 8 to 10 minutes. Remove the potatoes with a slotted spoon and transfer to a platter.

4. Add the salmon to the saucepan, reduce the heat to low, and simmer gently just until firm, about 4 minutes; transfer the salmon to the platter with the potatoes.

5. Add the cream to the saucepan and simmer over medium-low heat, stirring frequently, until reduced by about one-quarter, 15 to 20 minutes (don't let it boil over!).

6. In the meantime, make the puff pastry rounds: Preheat the oven to 400°F. On a lightly floured surface, roll out the chilled puff pastry ⅛ inch thick. Using a 6-inch bowl or plate as a template, cut out 8 rounds. Use a sharp knife to cut a 1-inch long slit in the center of each circle, then carefully transfer the puff pastry rounds to a large baking sheet and refrigerate them until well chilled.

7. In a small bowl, use a fork to blend the butter and flour into a smooth paste. Whisk the flour paste into the simmering soup a little at a time, and keep simmering until the soup is smooth and slightly thickened. Keep cooking and stirring for about 3 minutes more to cook off the taste of the flour.

8. Add the celery root mixture, potatoes, and salmon. Bring to a gentle simmer and cook for about 2 minutes more, just to warm through. Stir in the dill, parsley, lemon zest, lemon juice, salt, and pepper.

9. Ladle the chowder into eight 1¼-cup ovenproof bowls and scatter with a little of the cooked bacon. Lightly brush the rim of each bowl with a little of the egg wash and carefully top each bowl with a puff pastry round. Gently press the pastry around the edges of the bowls to seal. Brush the pastry with the egg wash and set the bowls on a large rimmed baking sheet. Bake the pot pies for 20 to 25 minutes, or until the tops are golden brown and puffed and the filling is bubbling. Serve immediately.

Avocado Soup with Lime Cream and Seared Chipotle Shrimp

This is a refreshing and delicious summer supper, and I like to make it easy on myself by preparing both the soup and the shrimp a day in advance and chilling them, separately of course, until I'm ready to serve the meal. For a memorable presentation, ladle the soup into stemless wineglasses, and then top with the cream and the shrimp. You can serve the glasses individually, or, if you're entertaining, you might put the wineglasses on a white platter and set it out as part of a buffet.

Serves 8

FOR THE SOUP

- 1 quart (4 cups) chicken broth, homemade or store-bought
- 4 medium ripe avocados, peeled, pitted, and chopped (about 3 cups)
- 2 tablespoons finely chopped fresh cilantro
- 2 tablespoons lime juice
- Coarse salt and freshly ground pepper

FOR THE LIME CREAM

- ¾ cup sour cream
- 1 tablespoon finely chopped fresh cilantro
- 1 teaspoon finely grated lime zest
- Coarse salt and freshly ground pepper

FOR THE SEARED CHIPOTLE SHRIMP

- 1 pound medium shrimp, peeled, deveined, and tails left on (31 to 40 count)
- ½ teaspoon ground cumin
- ½ teaspoon freshly ground pepper
- ¼ teaspoon coarse salt
- 1 tablespoon extra-virgin olive oil
- 1 cup fresh or thawed frozen corn kernels
- 1 garlic clove, minced

- 1 canned chipotle chili pepper in adobo sauce, finely chopped, plus 1 tablespoon of the sauce from the can (save the rest for another use)
- 1 tablespoon lime juice

1. **TO MAKE THE SOUP:** In a blender or food processor, puree the broth, avocados, cilantro, and lime juice until smooth. Season with salt and pepper, then chill the soup, covered, in the refrigerator for at least three hours or overnight.

2. **TO MAKE THE LIME CREAM:** In a medium nonreactive bowl, combine the sour cream, cilantro, lime zest, and salt and pepper to taste. Stir well to combine. Cover with plastic wrap and refrigerate until ready to use.

3. **TO MAKE THE SEARED CHIPOTLE SHRIMP:** Thoroughly pat the shrimp dry with paper towels. Season on both sides with the cumin, pepper, and salt.

4. In a large nonstick skillet over medium-high heat, pour in the oil. Add the shrimp and cook until heated through, about 2 minutes per side. Add the corn and garlic to the skillet, and cook, stirring, until the vegetables are softened, about 2 minutes more. Add the chipotle chili, adobo sauce, and lime juice, and continue to cook until the shrimp is golden and the corn is tender, about 2 minutes more.

5. To serve, ladle ¾ cup of soup into each bowl (or glass) and then top each with 1 tablespoon of the lime cream. Divide the shrimp and corn mixture evenly among the 6 bowls and serve immediately.

Gazpacho with BLT Sandwiches

Chilled fresh gazpacho is cooling and delicious when served on a hot summer night. For this gazpacho, try to dice the vegetables tiny—about ⅛ inch if possible. They stay crunchy and the flavors meld better. You can use all V8 spicy veggie juice if you cannot find the organic R. W. Knudsen. Note that classic BLTs are best served in the summer when tomatoes are fresh from the garden. Be sure to assemble yours just before eating!

Serves 8

For the Soup

One   32-ounce jar R. W. Knudsen Very Veggie juice

Two   16-ounce cans V8 juice

5   medium to large tomatoes, peeled, seeded, and finely diced (about 5 cups)

1   large orange bell pepper, finely diced (about ½ cup)

1   large red bell pepper, finely diced (about ½ cup)

1   large yellow bell pepper, finely diced (about ½ cup)

1   medium red or Vidalia onion, finely diced (about ½ cup)

2   large English cucumbers, peeled, seeded, and finely diced (about 4 cups)

¼   cup finely chopped fresh basil plus 8 leaves, for garnish

¼   cup extra-virgin olive oil

2   teaspoons finely grated lemon zest

3   tablespoons lemon juice, or more to taste

1   small jalapeño chile pepper, seeded and minced (about 1 tablespoon)

1   tablespoon sugar

2   large garlic cloves, minced

Coarse salt and freshly ground pepper

Hot sauce (optional)

For the Sandwiches

8   slices high-fiber whole-grain bread, such as 18-grain bread or quinoa bread

Mayonnaise, to taste

8 to 10 slices bacon, cooked

Bibb lettuce or arugula

2   medium tomatoes, sliced

Coarse salt and freshly ground pepper

1. **TO MAKE THE SOUP:** In a large bowl, combine the juices, tomatoes, bell peppers, onion, cucumbers, basil, oil, lemon zest, lemon juice, jalapeño, sugar, and garlic. Season with salt and pepper to taste, and a dash or two of hot sauce, if using. Cover the bowl and chill the soup for at least 3 hours before serving.

2. **TO MAKE THE SANDWICHES:** Toast the bread and spread with mayonnaise. Divide the bacon among 4 slices of bread. Top with the lettuce and tomato slices. Add a pinch of salt and a grind of pepper to the tomato. Top with the remaining 4 slices of bread. Cut each sandwich in half along the diagonal. Serve the soup in stemless wineglasses, with a leaf of basil on top of each and a sandwich half alongside.

TIP

TO PEEL TOMATOES: Bring a saucepan three-quarters full of water to a boil. Cut a very shallow cross in the smooth end of the tomatoes and drop them into the boiling water (if peeling more than four tomatoes, it's easier to do this in two batches). After 20 seconds, scoop up the tomatoes with a slotted spoon, transfer to a colander, and set under cool running water to stop them from cooking further. With a small sharp knife, peel the skin.

TO SEED CUCUMBERS: Halve the peeled cucumber lengthwise. Place the tip of a small spoon at the top of the seed channel, press in firmly, and scrape downward, scooping out the seeds.

SIMPLY OVEN BAKED

When I hear the word "roast," my thoughts run to the time when fall and winter roll around and there's nothing better than being in a warm, comforting kitchen on a cold, gloomy day—the whole house gets extra heat from the work of the oven, and savory smells from whatever's cooking perfume the air.

In the 1950s and 1960s, dinner often involved a roast served alongside a starch and a vegetable. That seems like a fairly old-fashioned idea of what a meal should be, especially when you consider the various foams and emulsions and exotic ingredients a lot of today's chefs favor. But while we may be inspired by the creative fare we see in restaurants, when it comes to what we cook at home for our families, there just may be some humble wisdom in the way our moms made dinner.

I think that the notion of a meal centered on an oven-baked dish, like a roast, is worth revising and updating, and that's what I've sought to do in this chapter. So these are not your mother's old-fashioned recipes for roasts and other baked dishes, and there's no advice to take a piece of meat and "set it in broiler until it's done" to be found. Instead I offer modern versions of the classics.

And here's what you'll like best: Not only is there something inherently comforting about a baked dish, but you'll realize that as soon as you put it in the oven you've freed up a lot of time to do the other things you love. So bake, roast, and slow cook your way to a delicious meal with the Wallace family favorites in this chapter. *Start your ovens!*

BEEF STROGANOFF, WAGSHAL'S FAMOUS

From the kitchen of Wagshal's executive chef, Ann Marie James

Wagshal's is an institution in Washington, D.C. The delicatessen has been in operation since 1925 and has been patronized by every president since Truman, hence its nickname, "the presidents' deli." The Wallaces are big fans, too, especially of the prepared foods from the store's executive chef, Ann Marie James—her beef stroganoff is a favorite.

Serves 8

- 4 tablespoons (½ stick) unsalted butter
- 2 large yellow onions, coarsely chopped (about 4 cups)
- 2 pounds button mushrooms, thinly sliced (about 3½ cups)
- 5 pounds sirloin tip or boneless sirloin steak, thinly sliced across the grain and cut into 1-inch pieces
- 1 quart (4 cups) veal stock or beef broth, homemade or store-bought, or more as needed to cover the beef
- ⅔ cup finely chopped fresh dill
- 2 teaspoons coarse salt, plus more to taste
- 2 teaspoons freshly ground pepper, plus more to taste
- 2 cups sour cream
- 1 pound wide egg noodles, cooked and buttered (optional), for serving

1. Preheat the oven to 350°F.

2. In a large Dutch oven over medium-high heat, melt 2 tablespoons of the butter. Add the onions and cook, stirring, until translucent, about 3 minutes. Add the mushrooms and cook until the liquid is released yet the mushrooms are still firm, 5 to 7 minutes. Transfer the onions and mushrooms to a medium bowl; set aside.

3. Heat the remaining 2 tablespoons butter in the same pan over high heat. Working in batches, sear the beef strips until brown, 3 to 4 minutes. Add the mushroom mixture. Add the stock, half of the dill, and the salt and pepper.

4. Cover tightly with a lid or foil and bake until the beef is fork-tender, 45 to 60 minutes. Remove from the oven and stir in the sour cream until well blended. Add the remaining dill and adjust the seasoning with additional salt and pepper, if needed. Serve over the buttered egg noodles, if you like.

CHICKEN WITH HONEY MUSTARD, APPLES, AND PEARS

Sliced apples and pears add sweetness to the savory sauce in this dish. It's perfect for a weeknight supper—the kind for which you usually don't make a dessert. If you're a white-meat person, replace the chicken thighs with halved bone-in chicken breasts.

Serves 8

- 3 pounds bone-in chicken thighs (8 large thighs or 16 small thighs), trimmed of excess fat
  Coarse salt and freshly ground pepper
- ¼ cup extra-virgin olive oil
- 2 large yellow onions, cut into wedges
- 2 medium cooking apples, such as Cortland, Granny Smith, or Macoun, cored and cut into 8 wedges each
- 2 medium cooking pears, such as Bosc or Anjou, cored and cut into 8 wedges each
- 2 cups chicken broth, homemade or store-bought
- ½ cup honey mustard
- 2 tablespoons all-purpose flour (optional)
- 1 tablespoon unsalted butter, softened (optional)
- ¼ cup finely chopped fresh flat-leaf parsley or 1 tablespoon dried (optional)

1. Preheat the oven to 450°F.

2. Wash the chicken thighs and pat them dry with paper towels. Season the thighs liberally all over with salt and pepper.

3. Heat the oil in a large ovenproof skillet over medium-high heat. Working in batches, add the thighs, skin-side down, and cook until golden, about 6 minutes. Flip the thighs and cook for 2 to 3 minutes longer.

4. Transfer the chicken to a plate and pour off all but 2 tablespoons of the drippings from the pan. Add the onion, apple, and pear wedges to the skillet and season with salt and pepper. Cook until the onions and fruit are slightly softened, stirring occasionally and gently, about 4 minutes.

5. In a medium nonreactive bowl, whisk together the broth and the mustard. Pour the mixture into the skillet and bring to a boil. As soon as it reaches a boil, use tongs to arrange the thighs skin-side up in the skillet, and transfer it to the oven. Roast until the thighs are cooked through, about 20 minutes. If this is a busy weeknight, serve the roasted chicken right from the skillet.

6. If you'd like something a bit more elaborate: While the chicken is cooking, in a small bowl combine the flour and butter to form a paste. When the chicken is done, use a slotted spoon to transfer the thighs and onion, apple, and pear wedges to a serving platter and cover loosely with foil to keep warm. Bring the pan juices in the skillet to a simmer over medium heat. Whisk in about half of the paste and bring to a boil. Thicken over a low boil, whisking constantly, about 2 minutes. Continue to whisk, adding more of the paste as needed to make a rich, slightly thick pan sauce. Pour the sauce over the chicken, onion, apples, and pears, garnish with a sprinkle of parsley if you like, and serve.

CHICKEN BAKED WITH TOMATOES AND HERBS

If you like tangy chicken coated with barbecue sauce but don't relish all the sugar that is often in those bottled sauces, try this simple oven-baked version made by combining tomato puree and evaporated milk instead. To save time, you can prepare the chicken up to the point where you cover it with the tomato sauce, refrigerate it up to 4 hours or overnight, then top it with the bread crumbs and melted butter right before you're ready to cook and eat the dish—it will be even more rich and savory. Just remember to allow it to come to room temperature before baking.

Serves 8

- 8 pounds bone-in, skin-on chicken (4 whole breasts plus 5 or so whole legs)
- 1 cup evaporated milk
- 1 cup tomato puree
- 6 tablespoons unsalted butter, melted
- 1 tablespoon coarse salt
- 2 teaspoons freshly ground pepper
- 4 scallions, white and tender green parts only, coarsely chopped (about ½ cup)
- 6 garlic cloves, peeled
- 2 tablespoons apple cider vinegar
- 1 teaspoon fresh thyme or ⅓ teaspoon dried
- ¾ cup plain dried bread crumbs

1. Wash the chicken pieces and pat them dry with paper towels. Using a cleaver, split the breasts in half. Let the chicken come to room temperature for 15 minutes.

2. Position two racks in the upper portion of the oven and preheat the oven to 375°F.

3. In a medium nonreactive bowl, whisk to combine the evaporated milk, ketchup, 3 tablespoons of the melted butter, the salt, and pepper. Set aside.

4. Line 2 large baking sheets with aluminum foil and place the breasts on one sheet and the legs on the other.

5. In a small food processor, combine the scallions, garlic, vinegar, and thyme and pulse several times until finely chopped. Using your hands, rub the herb mixture evenly on each chicken piece and let stand for 10 minutes.

6. Cover the chicken with the tomato sauce mixture, and let it stand for another 30 minutes.

7. Sprinkle the bread crumbs evenly over the chicken pieces and drizzle the remaining melted butter on top of each piece of chicken. Bake for 30 minutes, then rotate the baking sheets and continue to cook until the sauce is bubbly and the chicken is golden, 35 to 40 minutes more. Remove the chicken from the oven and let cool about 10 minutes. Serve the chicken pieces piled on a large platter.

CHICKEN PARMESAN BAKE

From the kitchen of Ricky Lauren

Every year we go to Jamaica over the winter holidays and often run into our dear friends, Ricky and Ralph Lauren. In addition to being an artist and an extremely creative person, Ricky is an excellent home cook and a fellow cookbook author. This is one of her family's favorite dishes, one they would eat at the beach on weekends—piled on a large platter with angel hair pasta on the side. "Even though I make an enormous amount, it never lasts through the weekend!" Ricky says. Funnily enough, Ricky doesn't call for Parmigiano Reggiano cheese in her version of this Italian classic, but when I make it I like to combine 1 cup grated Parmesan with the panko crumbs and I encourage you to try it this way too. You could also serve this dish with freshly grated Parmesan, if you like.

Serves 8

Nonstick cooking spray

1 cup all-purpose flour

Coarse salt and freshly ground pepper

Hungarian paprika, to taste

Garlic salt, such as Lawry's, to taste

2 large eggs, beaten

1½ cups panko bread crumbs

2 whole chickens, cut into 10 pieces (about 7 pounds total)

1 pound mozzarella cheese, thinly sliced

2 cups tomato sauce, homemade or store-bought

1. Preheat the oven to 350°F.

2. Spray a roasting pan or baking dish large enough to hold the chicken with nonstick cooking spray. Mix the flour, salt and pepper, paprika, and garlic salt together in a shallow bowl. Put the eggs and panko in two additional shallow bowls. Dredge the chicken pieces, one at a time, first in the flour, then in the eggs, and last in the panko. Place the pieces in the roasting pan. Bake, turning the chicken when the bottom side is brown, until golden on both sides, 30 to 35 minutes.

3 . Place the sliced mozzarella on top of the chicken and pour the tomato sauce on top. Continue to bake until the cheese has melted and the sauce is piping hot. Place the chicken on a large platter and serve.

CHICKEN THIGHS WITH ROASTED CAULIFLOWER

This is a truly easy-to-make and very versatile recipe. For instance, if you're not a huge cauliflower fan, just substitute broccoli. You can swap out the lime juice and crushed red pepper flakes for lemon juice and parsley if you like.

Serves 8

- 4½ pounds bone-in chicken thighs (about 10)
- Coarse salt and freshly ground pepper
- 1 tablespoon extra-virgin olive oil
- 1 large head cauliflower, cut into small florets (about 1½ pounds)
- ¼ teaspoon crushed red pepper flakes
- 1 tablespoon lime juice
- ½ cup loosely packed fresh cilantro leaves

1. Wash the chicken thighs and pat them dry with paper towels. Season the thighs with salt and pepper on both sides, and allow to stand at room temperature for 15 minutes.

2. Preheat the oven to 450°F.

3. In a large ovenproof skillet over medium-high heat, heat the oil. Cook the thighs, skin-side down, until they are crisp and golden-brown, about 3 minutes. Turn the thighs and continue to cook until crispy on the other side, 3 to 4 minutes more. Transfer the thighs to a plate.

4. To the same skillet, add the cauliflower, red pepper flakes, and a pinch of salt and pepper. Toss to combine and coat with the pan juices. Nestle the chicken thighs skin-side up in the cauliflower in the skillet.

5. Transfer the skillet to the oven and roast until the cauliflower is tender and the chicken is cooked through, 20 to 25 minutes.

6. Remove the pan from the oven. Pour the lime juice over the chicken and cauliflower and stir it in along with the cilantro leaves. Serve immediately from the skillet.

CORNISH HENS WITH LEMON-CHILI GLAZE

Cornish hens are so simple to make and so festive. They manage to be both quaint and impressive at the same time, and look especially beautiful on the plate when served with wild rice.

Serves 8

Four 1½-pound Cornish game hens (not frozen), halved lengthwise along the breast

Coarse salt and freshly ground pepper

1 cup lemon juice

8 garlic cloves, pressed

¼ cup extra-virgin olive oil

⅔ cup unsalted butter

1 teaspoon Tabasco sauce

½ teaspoon crushed red pepper flakes

Fresh parsley sprigs (optional), for garnish

1. Wash the hens and pat them dry with paper towels. Season generously inside and out with salt and pepper. Add the hen halves to a large plastic bag along with the lemon juice and garlic, seal the bag completely, and massage to coat the hens in the marinade. Refrigerate for at least 6 hours or overnight.

2. Bring the hens to room temperature 1 hour before baking.

3. Preheat the oven to 425°F.

4. Rub the hen halves all over with the oil and place them in a baking dish large enough to hold them firmly.

5. In a small saucepan over medium heat, melt the butter and whisk in the Tabasco sauce and red pepper flakes to combine. Reduce the heat to low and simmer until thick and syrupy, about 10 minutes. Pour the sauce over the hens. Roast the hens until cooked through, about 35 minutes. Transfer the hens to a warm platter and let rest, loosely covered with foil, for 10 minutes. Garnish with the parsley sprigs before serving, if you like.

DUCK BREASTS ROASTED WITH CHINESE SPICES

Duck has many advantages: Its meat is darker and richer, with more natural flavor and fat, than chicken. The slightly gamy flavor of duck breasts pairs well with the piquant Chinese spices here. This dish is excellent served with steamed rice and roasted Brussels sprouts.

Serves 8

- 2 teaspoons coarse salt
- 1 cup soy sauce
- 2 tablespoons dark brown sugar
- 2 tablespoons dry sherry
- 2 tablespoons honey
- 2 tablespoons creamy or crunchy peanut butter
- 1 tablespoon seasoned rice vinegar
- 2 large garlic cloves, minced
- 1 tablespoon dark sesame oil
- 1 teaspoon Chinese five-spice powder
- ½ teaspoon cayenne pepper
- Eight 5- to 6-ounce boneless duck breast halves, fat trimmed

1. Combine everything but the duck in a medium bowl to make the marinade; whisk to blend. Place the duck breasts, skin-side up, on a cutting board. Using a sharp knife, score lines, ½ inch apart, in a crosshatch pattern into the fat; cut almost all the way through, but do not cut into the flesh. Transfer breasts to a jumbo plastic bag and pour in the marinade. Seal the bag; turn to coat the duck. Refrigerate for 2 days, turning occasionally.

2. Preheat the oven to 400°F.

3. Drain the duck well, discarding the marinade. Place the breasts, skin-side down, in a cold medium skillet. Place over medium-high heat and cook until most of the fat has rendered and the skin is dark golden brown, 5 to 8 minutes. Transfer the duck breasts, skin-side up, to a rimmed baking sheet. Roast until cooked to desired doneness, 3 to 5 minutes for small duck breasts and 8 to 10 minutes for large duck breasts, or until a meat thermometer inserted into the thickest part of the duck registers 125°F. Remove from the oven and let rest, covered loosely with foil, for 10 minutes. Transfer the duck breasts to a cutting board. Thinly slice each breast crosswise on a slight diagonal and serve.

TIP
Chicken will also work in this recipe: Substitute four 12-ounce boneless, skin-on chicken breast halves for the duck, and don't score the breasts. To cook, heat 2 teaspoons oil in a large skillet over medium heat; cook until golden brown, about 10 minutes. Flip chicken, and transfer to the oven. Cook until chicken reaches 175°F, about 25 minutes.

FISH WITH TERIYAKI GLAZE AND ASIAN CUCUMBER SALAD

The basic teriyaki sauce in this recipe is so versatile: You can whip up a batch and use it for glazing a whole host of proteins besides fish; it's especially good for chicken or shrimp. I also often broil salmon for several minutes and then spoon this sauce on top to finish for a quick weeknight meal.

Serves 8

- 2 small English cucumbers, thinly sliced (about 3 cups)
- 2 small daikon radishes, peeled and thinly sliced, or 2 small jicama, peeled and thinly sliced (about 1 cup)
- 2 garlic cloves, minced
- 1 cup unseasoned rice vinegar
- ¼ cup sugar
- 2 teaspoons coarse salt
- ¾ cup soy sauce
- ½ cup light brown sugar
- 1 tablespoon cornstarch dissolved in 2 tablespoons water
- 8 skinless fillets of firm-fleshed fish such as cod, halibut, or salmon
- 4 cups steamed jasmine rice (optional), for serving

1. Place the cucumbers, daikon, and garlic in a medium nonreactive bowl and set aside. In a small saucepan, combine ½ cup of the vinegar with the sugar and salt. Cook over low heat, stirring constantly, just until the sugar and salt dissolve. Pour the mixture over the vegetables, cover, and chill in the refrigerator. Save the saucepan.

2. Preheat the broiler and position a rack 6 inches from the heat. Line a large baking sheet with aluminum foil.

3. In the same saucepan you used to heat the rice vinegar mixture, combine the soy sauce, brown sugar, cornstarch mixture, and the remaining ½ cup vinegar and bring to a boil, whisking constantly until the glaze is thickened, about 2 minutes. Remove the glaze from the heat. Line the fish fillets on the prepared baking sheet. Brush each fillet with the glaze on both sides, reserving a small amount of the glaze for basting. Broil the fish for 5 minutes, remove the baking sheet from the oven, baste the fillets, then return them to the broiler and cook them through, about 5 minutes more.

4. To serve, use a slotted spoon to transfer the cucumber salad to the plates next to the fish, drizzle any of the remaining glaze over the fish, and serve ½ cup steamed jasmine rice alongside, if you like.

Flank Steak with Romesco Sauce

I adore romesco sauce, the oil-and-red-pepper–based condiment from Catalonia, Spain. It's not only wildly flavorful, but it's also a lot healthier than some of the rich butter-based sauces often offered with steaks. Although in Spain this sauce is mostly used on fish and poultry, I've found that it pairs beautifully with red meat, too—especially toothsome flank steak.

Serves 8

4	slices whole-grain bread, torn into 2-inch pieces
¼	cup sliced almonds
2	tablespoons extra-virgin olive oil
2	garlic cloves, minced
½	teaspoon smoked paprika
Two	7-ounce jars roasted red peppers, drained
2	tablespoons sherry vinegar
1	teaspoon coarse salt, plus more to taste
Two	1½-pound flank steaks
	Freshly ground pepper

1. Preheat the broiler and position the rack in the upper portion of the oven.

2. Arrange the bread and almonds on a baking sheet in a single layer. Broil until lightly browned, about 1 minute. Transfer immediately to a food processor and process until the bread and almonds are coarsely ground.

3. Heat the oil, garlic, and paprika in a medium skillet over medium heat. Cook until the garlic begins to brown, about 1 minute. Add the garlic mixture, roasted peppers, vinegar, and salt to the almond-bread mixture and process until smooth. Scrape the sauce from the processor, cover, and set aside.

4. Season the steaks with salt and pepper. Lightly oil a large heavy broiling pan and place the steaks on it. Broil the steaks for 5 minutes per side for medium rare, or until they reach the desired doneness. Transfer the steaks to a cutting board, cover loosely with foil, and let rest for 10 minutes.

5. Thinly slice the meat against the grain and serve with the sauce.

POT ROAST, SLOWLY BRAISED

From the kitchen of Kelly Alexander

My friend the food writer Kelly Alexander swears by her late grandmother Lil Pachter's pot roast and has shared with me the fondest memories of her Mema making it on Friday night dinners and for special family events and all the Jewish holidays. She says that the pot roast is best the second day, after the flavors have really had a chance to meld, so if possible, try to make this the day before your family plans to enjoy it.

Serves 8

- 1 tablespoon Hungarian paprika
- 1 tablespoon freshly ground pepper
- 1 tablespoon coarse salt
- 2 teaspoons dried oregano
- One 5-pound beef brisket, trimmed of some of its fat
- 3 tablespoons vegetable oil
- 3½ cups chicken stock, homemade or store-bought
- One 14.5-ounce can diced tomatoes, juices reserved
- 2 bay leaves
- 3 medium yellow onions, thinly sliced (about 2 cups)
- 3 garlic cloves, finely chopped

1. Preheat the oven to 350°F. Combine the paprika, pepper, salt, and oregano in a small bowl, then rub all over the brisket.

2. In an ovenproof enameled cast-iron pot or other heavy pot with a tight-fitting lid, just large enough to hold the brisket snugly, heat the oil over medium-high heat. Add the brisket to the pot and brown on both sides, about 10 minutes per side. Transfer the brisket to a platter and pour off the fat from the pot. Add the stock, tomatoes, and bay leaves and use a wooden spoon to scrape up any browned bits stuck to the bottom of the pot. Return the brisket and any accumulated juices to the pot and scatter the onions and garlic over the meat. Cover the pot, transfer to the oven, and braise for 1 hour. Uncover the pot and continue to braise for another hour.

3. Push some of the onions and garlic into the braising liquid surrounding the brisket. Cover the pot, return it to the oven, and continue to braise until the meat is very tender, up to 2 hours more. Check the meat for doneness occasionally during cooking by piercing the brisket with a sharp knife; when fully cooked, the knife should slide in easily.

4. Transfer the brisket to a cutting board and loosely cover with foil. The onions and garlic in the pot should be very soft and the braising juices should be rich and saucy. If the juices are too thin, transfer the pot to the stovetop and simmer over medium heat until the juices thicken, about 5 minutes. Slice the brisket across the grain and transfer to a warm serving platter. Spoon the tomatoes, onions, garlic, and sauce on top. Discard the bay leaves before serving.

MEAT LOAF WITH HERB GRAVY, DOWN-HOME STYLE

The technique of poking small holes in the top of the meat loaf and pouring a little water into them ensures even cooking, prevents the meat loaf from drying out, and yields more golden juice to make a gravy if you like.

Makes 2 loaves, serves 8

FOR THE MEAT LOAVES

Nonstick cooking spray

2 large eggs

¼ cup tomato paste

Coarse salt and freshly ground pepper

1 cup beef broth, homemade or store-bought

2 pounds ground beef chuck

2 pounds ground pork

2 cups plain dried bread crumbs

4 medium celery stalks, finely chopped (about 2 cups)

2 medium yellow onions, finely chopped (about 1½ cups)

½ cup finely chopped fresh flat-leaf parsley or 2 tablespoons dried

1 tablespoon dried rosemary

FOR THE GRAVY

8 tablespoons (1 stick) unsalted butter

½ cup all-purpose flour

1 quart (4 cups) beef broth, or strain some of the meat loaf's pan juices and combine with enough beef broth to make 4 cups of liquid

1 tablespoon dried ground sage

Coarse salt and freshly ground pepper

1. **TO MAKE THE MEAT LOAVES:** Preheat the oven to 350°F. Lightly spray two 9 × 5-inch loaf pans with cooking spray.

2. In a medium bowl, whisk the eggs with the tomato paste and salt and pepper until well combined. Whisk in the broth. Using your hands, work in the ground beef and pork along with the bread crumbs, celery, onions, parsley, and rosemary and combine; take care not to overmix. Divide the mixture evenly and pack into the prepared pans. Using a butter knife or the handle of a wooden spoon, poke 6 holes in each meatloaf, as evenly spaced as you can make them, and pour just a little water into each. Bake the meat loaves on a rack in the center of the oven until an instant-read thermometer inserted into the center of a loaf registers 165°F, 1 to 1½ hours. Gently and carefully drain the juices out of the meat loaf pans into a glass measuring cup or gravy separator, and set aside. Cover the loaves loosely with foil to keep warm and let rest while you make the gravy.

3. **TO MAKE THE GRAVY:** In a medium saucepan over low heat, melt the butter. Whisk in the flour, and cook, whisking constantly to combine, for 1 minute. Slowly whisk in the pan juices and the broth, a little at time, to combine. While whisking constantly, raise the heat to medium and allow the gravy to just come to a boil; as soon as it reaches a boil, reduce the heat to medium-low and simmer until slightly thickened and reduced, about 5 minutes. Strain the gravy through a mesh sieve into a bowl. Stir in the sage, and season to taste with salt and pepper.

4. To serve, pour the gravy into a warmed sauceboat, cut the meat loaf into thick slices and place on a warmed platter, and pass them together.

OSSO BUCO WITH GREMOLATA

This is a terrific dish for supper on a cold winter night. Most Italians would serve this with a creamy risotto, but I think it is also delicious with polenta or whipped potatoes. Do make the extra effort to prepare the gremolata for that special fresh herb taste and presentation.

The flavor of this dish only improves if it's made in advance. It may be refrigerated in its sauce, covered tightly with a lid, for up to 3 days before serving. When ready to serve, let the dish come to room temperature for about 2 hours and then bring to a gentle simmer over medium-high heat until fully rewarmed; you may need to add a little more liquid to the pot before reheating.

Serves 8

FOR THE OSSO BUCO

- 6 sprigs fresh thyme
- 1 large sprig fresh rosemary
- 2 bay leaves
- 8 meaty veal shanks (6 to 7 pounds total), tied
- ¾ cup all-purpose flour
  Coarse salt and freshly ground pepper
- ½ cup extra-virgin olive oil
- 3 medium leeks, white and tender green parts only, sliced ¼ inch thick (about 2 cups)
- 2 large carrots, peeled and diced ¼ inch thick (about 1 cup)
- 2 medium celery stalks, diced (about 1 cup)
- 1 medium yellow onion, finely chopped (about ⅔ cup)
- 4 garlic cloves, smashed
  Finely grated zest of 1 medium lemon (about 1 tablespoon)
- 2 cups dry white or red wine, or a combination
- 2 cups chicken broth, homemade or store-bought

FOR THE GREMOLATA

- 1½ cups finely chopped fresh flat-leaf parsley
- 2 tablespoons finely grated lemon zest
- 2 garlic cloves, minced
  Crushed red pepper flakes
- 2 cups cooked polenta or whipped potatoes, for serving

1. **TO MAKE THE OSSO BUCO:** Preheat the oven to 350°F and position the rack in the center of the oven.

2. To make a bouquet garni, place the sprigs of thyme and rosemary and the bay leaves in the center of a small square of cheesecloth. Fold the cloth around the herbs to form a pouch, then secure tightly with a knot or kitchen twine. Set aside.

3. Rinse the veal shanks and pat them dry using paper towels. Pour the flour into a large shallow plate and season it with salt and pepper. Dredge the shanks in the seasoned flour, coating them evenly and lightly shaking off excess flour.

4. In a large ovenproof stockpot or Dutch oven, heat the oil over medium-high heat. Working in batches, add the veal and brown the shanks on both sides, 4 to 6 minutes per side, adding a little more oil if necessary. Transfer the browned shanks to a large baking sheet to rest while you finish browning all of the meat. Lightly season the tops of the shanks with salt and pepper and let rest.

continued on page 60

continued from page 58

5. Add the leeks, carrots, celery, and onion to the pot and continue to cook over medium-high heat until the vegetables are softened, 6 to 8 minutes. Add the garlic and lemon zest and continue to cook for another minute, stirring. Add the wine and deglaze the pan, scraping up any brown bits from the bottom. Add the bouquet garni and the broth. Return the shanks to the pot and bring the mixture to a simmer.

6. Cover the pot with a lid and place in the oven. Braise until the shanks are fork-tender and meltingly soft, 2½ to 3 hours.

7. **TO MAKE THE GREMOLATA:** In a small bowl, toss together the parsley, lemon zest, garlic, and pinch of red pepper flakes.

8. To serve, mound a couple of tablespoons of polenta or whipped potatoes onto each plate and then gently transfer a veal shank atop each one, ladling the jus and vegetables remaining in the pot over the meat. Garnish each with a tablespoon of gremolata. Serve with a thin marrow fork or spoon for scooping out the shank's delicious marrow.

NOTE
Ask your butcher for 8 veal shanks of similar size, each of them tied around the middle (like a belt) so the meat is secured to the bone and holds its shape during cooking; you can also tie them yourself.

Salmon Charbroiled on a Bed of Baby Bok Choy

Many people are trying to get more salmon—a so-called super food—into their diets, and in the Wallace household we are no exception. This preparation is an easy way to load up on Omega-3s because the fish and bok choy are cooked quickly under the broiler, all in one dish.

Serves 8

- ½ cup soy sauce
- ¼ cup honey
- 1 tablespoon dark sesame oil
- 1 tablespoon peeled grated fresh ginger
- 1 teaspoon garlic powder
- 2 pounds baby bok choy, well rinsed, bottoms trimmed, and halved lengthwise
- Eight 6-ounce skin-on salmon fillets
- ½ cup clam juice or fish broth
- 1 bunch scallions, white and tender green parts only, thinly sliced on the diagonal (about ¾ cup)

1. Preheat the broiler and position the rack in the upper portion of the oven.

2. In a medium nonreactive bowl, combine the soy sauce, honey, oil, ginger, and garlic powder and whisk to combine. Set aside.

3. In a 13 × 9-inch casserole dish, arrange the bok choy in a single layer. Place the salmon fillets, skin-side down, on top of the bok choy. Pour half of the prepared sauce evenly over the salmon, and the rest over the bok choy in between the fillets. Broil the salmon for 5 minutes. Remove the salmon from the oven and stir the bok choy leaves between the salmon fillets to prevent them from sticking to the dish. Pour in the clam juice around the fish. Broil for an additional 2 minutes or until the salmon reaches the desired doneness.

4. To serve, arrange the bok choy on plates and top with the salmon fillets. Top each fillet with the scallions and serve immediately.

Pasticcio, Mediterranean "Mac 'n' Meat"

When our daughter Sarah was in fifth grade she had to write her first term paper, on Greece. After the papers were graded the class celebrated with a "Greek" lunch. I was handed a pasticcio recipe to bring for our potluck. Sarah loved it! Over the years I have perfected my own formula, and pasticcio remains the dish Sarah requests for her birthday to this day. Complete the supper with a Greek salad and toasted pita bread points, if you like.

Serves 8

FOR THE FILLING

- 4 tablespoons (½ stick) unsalted butter
- 1 large onion, finely chopped (about 1 cup)
- 2½ to 3 pounds ground lamb or beef, or a combination
- Coarse salt and freshly ground pepper
- Dash of ground cinnamon
- ½ cup water
- 2 tablespoons tomato paste
- 1 pound elbow macaroni
- 3 large eggs, beaten
- 1 pound cheddar cheese, grated (4 cups)

FOR THE CREAM SAUCE

- 6 tablespoons unsalted butter
- ¾ cup all-purpose flour
- 1 quart whole milk, warm
- 3 large eggs, beaten
- 2 teaspoons coarse salt

1. **TO MAKE THE FILLING:** Preheat the oven to 350°F. Generously grease a 13 × 9-inch casserole dish.

2. In a large heavy skillet over medium-high heat, melt the butter. Add the onion and cook, stirring, until golden, about 6 minutes. Add the meat and cook, stirring, until the meat is browned. Gently drain and discard the excess fat in the pan. Season with salt and pepper and add the cinnamon, then stir in the water and tomato paste and cook to thoroughly combine, about 5 minutes more.

3. Cook the macaroni to al dente according to the package directions. Drain the macaroni, immediately rinse it in cold water, pour it into a large nonreactive bowl, and set aside to cool slightly. When the macaroni is lukewarm, add the eggs and mix well. Season with salt. Set aside until ready to use.

4. **TO MAKE THE CREAM SAUCE:** Melt the butter in a medium saucepan over medium-low heat, then add the flour and cook, whisking constantly, until the mixture is golden, about 2 minutes. Gradually stir in the milk, whisking constantly, until the sauce is smooth and thickened, 10 to 12 minutes. Remove the sauce from the heat to cool. When the sauce is partially cooled, stir in the eggs and salt.

5. Pour half of the macaroni into the prepared baking dish and sprinkle generously with 1 cup of the cheese. Add the meat sauce on top of the cheese and sprinkle with another cup of the cheese. Repeat the process with the remaining macaroni, cheese, and meat sauce. Top with the remaining cheese and bake for 10 minutes.

6. After the casserole has baked for 10 minutes, remove it from the oven and top with the cream sauce, making indents with a fork to allow the sauce to mix into the macaroni and meat. Bake for 30 minutes longer or until well browned. Let the pasticcio rest for 10 minutes, then serve warm.

ROASTED CHICKEN THE MEDITERRANEAN WAY

A roasted chicken doesn't have to be one big bird; you can cut it up and roast the pieces just as easily, and that way all the pieces become evenly golden brown and flavored with whatever herbs and spices you might be using. This simple supper with vegetables and herbs from the Mediterranean—artichokes, capers, and oregano—starts in a skillet and then gets finished off in the oven.

Serves 8

Two 9-ounce packages frozen artichoke hearts

½ cup water

One 4-pound chicken, cut into 8 pieces, plus 2 bone-in split chicken breasts (10 pieces total)

Coarse salt and freshly ground pepper

½ cup extra-virgin olive oil

2 cups grape or cherry tomatoes, halved

4 tablespoons capers, with a little of their juice

1 tablespoon lemon juice

2 teaspoons dried oregano

2 garlic cloves, minced

Crushed red pepper flakes

1. Position a rack in the center of the oven and preheat the oven to 425°F.

2. Place the artichoke hearts in a medium saucepan and cover with the water. Bring to a boil over medium-high heat; reduce the heat to a simmer and cook for 5 to 6 minutes, stirring occasionally. Drain the hearts and set them aside to rest until ready to use.

3. Wash the chicken and pat dry using paper towels. Season the pieces with salt and pepper. Heat ¼ cup of the oil in a large skillet over medium-high heat. Working in batches, place the chicken in the skillet, skin-side down, and cook until well browned, 6 to 8 minutes. Flip the chicken and continue to brown, about 3 minutes longer. Transfer the chicken pieces, skin-side up, to a large deep baking dish or casserole. Add the cooked artichoke hearts to the skillet and cook, stirring occasionally and taking care to scrape up any browned bits in the pan, about 6 minutes. Stir in the tomatoes and capers to combine and continue to cook, stirring, until the tomatoes are just wilted, 4 to 6 minutes longer. Transfer the artichoke mixture under and around the chicken. Bake, uncovered, for 30 minutes.

4. Meanwhile, in a small bowl, whisk the remaining ¼ cup oil with the lemon juice, oregano, garlic, and red pepper flakes to taste. Drizzle the mixture over the chicken and vegetables and return to the oven to cook for 5 minutes longer. Remove the casserole from the oven and let stand 10 minutes. Serve the chicken and vegetables family style.

ROASTED CHICKEN THE FRENCH WAY

When I first met Chris, he let me know for one of our first homemade dinner dates that he loved roast chicken. I kept making chicken for him and he kept saying that the skin was not crispy enough. I asked our daughter Catherine, who was twelve years old at the time, what was he talking about, and she recommended that I purchase a book called Simply French *by Patricia Wells, which her mother used for a recipe called Grandmother's Roast Chicken, and I have relied on it ever since. Catherine prepares a chicken most Sunday evenings to enjoy and live off during her hectic week as an editor at HarperCollins.*

Serves 8

One 5-pound chicken

1½ tablespoons unsalted butter, softened

Coarse salt and freshly ground pepper

2 heads garlic, unpeeled and halved horizontally

1 large sprig fresh rosemary

1 large sprig fresh thyme

1. Preheat the oven to 425°F. Lightly grease a roasting pan.

2. Rub the skin of the chicken with the butter and season the bird generously inside and out with salt and pepper. Twist the chicken's wings behind the back and tie the legs together with kitchen string.

3. Place the chicken on its side in the prepared roasting pan. Alongside the chicken arrange the prepared garlic heads, cut-side up, rosemary, and thyme. Bake the chicken, uncovered, for 20 minutes. Remove the chicken from the oven, baste it with its accumulated pan juices, turn it over, and return to the oven. Roast, uncovered, for 20 minutes more.

4. Remove the chicken from the oven, baste it again, turn it breast-side up, return it to the oven, and roast for 20 minutes more. Reduce the heat to 375°F. Remove the chicken from the oven. Baste it again. Return it to the oven and roast until the juices run clear when you pierce a thigh with a skewer, about 15 minutes longer.

5. Remove the pan from the oven and season the chicken generously with salt and pepper. Transfer the chicken to a cutting board, reserving the pan with its juices. Place the chicken on the board against the edge of a plate, so that the head is down and the tail is elevated. Cover loosely with foil and let rest in this position for at least 10 but not longer than 30 minutes.

continued on page 68

continued from page 67

6. **MAKE THE SAUCE:** Place the roasting pan over medium heat and use a wooden spoon to scrape up any bits of chicken and skin clinging to the bottom. Cook, scraping and stirring constantly, until the accumulated liquid is golden brown with no hints of pink, 2 to 3 minutes, taking care not to let it burn. Using a spoon, skim off any excess fat. Add 3 to 4 tablespoons of water to the plan, depending on how much liquid you have, and bring the liquid to a boil. Reduce the heat to low and simmer until thickened, about 5 minutes.

7. While the sauce is thickening, carve the chicken and arrange it on a warm platter. Strain the sauce through a fine-mesh strainer and pour it into a warmed sauceboat, if you like. Serve the chicken immediately with the pan sauce and the halved heads of garlic.

SALMON PACKETS WITH SHIITAKES AND SPINACH

I prefer to use parchment paper to make my oven-roasted packets instead of aluminum foil because it is a more natural product. This is a recipe I use often for our weekly meals because it is a meal-in-one; everything you need fits into the packets. Just toss a salad and dinner is served!

Serves 8

     4 tablespoons reduced sodium soy sauce

     2 tablespoons honey

     2 teaspoons garlic powder

     3 tablespoons fresh lemon juice

Two 10-ounce containers sliced shiitake mushrooms

One 5-ounce bag baby spinach leaves

     8 boneless, skinless salmon fillets, about 6 ounces each

     8 teaspoons toasted sesame oil

1. Preheat the oven to 400°F. Cut eight 12- to 15-inch squares of parchment paper.

2. In a small bowl, whisk to combine the soy sauce, honey, garlic powder, and lemon juice.

3. In a large bowl, combine the mushrooms and spinach. Pour the soy vinaigrette over the vegetables and toss to coat.

4. Lay out the parchment squares. Divide the vegetable mixture evenly among the parchment squares. Lay 1 fish fillet atop the vegetables. Drizzle ½ teaspoon of the sesame oil on top of each piece of fish. Fold parchment over the ingredients to enclose and make overlapping pleats to seal well. (You can also fold over the long sides of the parchment together twice, then roll in the short sides to form a pouch)

5. Transfer the packets to a rimmed baking sheet and bake for 10 to 12 minutes (the fish should be slightly firm and opaque throughout). Gently remove the fish from the packages and transfer to warm plates. Serve immediately.

ARGENTINIAN-STYLE PORK SHOULDER WITH CHIMICHURRI SAUCE

The classic Argentinian condiment known as chimichurri sauce gets its distinctive dark green color from the combination of fresh cilantro and parsley. The herbs are enhanced with garlic and bound with oil. The result is a vibrant, piquant sauce that wakes up your palate and is utterly habit-forming.

Serves 8

FOR THE PORK ROAST

One 5-pound trimmed boneless pork shoulder, at room temperature

½ cup extra-virgin olive oil

2 tablespoons coarse salt

1 tablespoon onion powder

1 tablespoon garlic powder

1 tablespoon smoked paprika

FOR THE CHIMICHURRI SAUCE

1 cup packed fresh flat-leaf parsley leaves

½ cup packed fresh cilantro leaves

¼ cup lemon juice

¼ cup red wine vinegar

3 garlic cloves

1 teaspoon ground cumin

½ teaspoon crushed red pepper flakes

1 teaspoon salt

½ cup extra-virgin olive oil

1. **TO MAKE THE PORK ROAST:** Preheat the oven to 325°F.

2. Pat the pork shoulder dry thoroughly with paper towels.

3. In a small bowl, combine the oil with the salt, onion powder, garlic powder, and paprika. Using a boning knife, make a few deep slits in the meat. Rub the spice mixture all over the pork and in between the slits.

4. Set the pork roast in a large, heavy roasting pan, fat-side up. Roast, basting with the accumulated pan juices every 30 minutes, until an instant-read thermometer inserted in the thickest part of the meat registers 165°F, about 4 hours. Transfer to a carving board and loosely cover with foil to rest for 20 minutes.

5. **TO MAKE THE CHIMICHURRI SAUCE:** In a food processor, combine the parsley, cilantro, lemon juice, vinegar, garlic, cumin, red pepper flakes, and salt. Gradually pour in the oil. Process until well combined and smooth, about 3 minutes. Scrape the sauce into a bowl, cover, and let stand at room temperature until ready to serve.

6. When ready to serve, carve the pork into ½-inch-thick slices and arrange on a platter. Spread the chimichurri sauce around the slices, if you like, or serve in a bowl at the table alongside the pork.

Pitmaster-Style Oven Roasted Barbecue Pork

From the kitchen of Myron Mixon

Every spring on the mall they hold the National Capital Barbecue Battle, a wonderful three-day competition you should try to attend if you are here at that time of year. That is where I was lucky to meet Myron Mixon, aka the "Winningest Man in Barbecue," and get a signed copy of his book Smokin'. *Ever since then, my choice in barbecue sauce is Jack's Old South—a sauce Myron created to honor his dad Jack, who also was a pitmaster. Go to his web site* www.jacksoldsouth.com *to try it for yourself. Here he shares his foolproof pork shoulder recipe, and I promise you will love it as much as the Wallace household does!*

Serves 8

- 3 cups apple juice
- 1 cup white vinegar
- ¾ cup white sugar
- ¾ cup plus 2 tablespoons coarse salt
- One 5-pound trimmed boneless pork shoulder, at room temperature
- 1 cup packed light brown sugar
- 2 tablespoons chili powder
- 2 tablespoons dry mustard
- 2 tablespoons onion powder
- 2 tablespoons garlic powder
- 2 tablespoons freshly ground pepper
- 2 teaspoons cayenne pepper

1. In a large, heavy saucepan over medium heat, combine the apple juice and vinegar. Whisking continuously, pour in the white sugar and ¾ cup salt. Continue cooking, whisking constantly, until the sugar and salt are completely dissolved, but do not allow the mixture to come to a boil. Remove the pan from the heat and let the marinade cool completely.

2. Place the pork shoulder in a large aluminum roasting pan, add the cooled marinade, cover with plastic wrap, and marinate in the refrigerator for at least 3 hours or overnight.

3. Preheat the oven to 300°F.

4. Remove the meat from the marinade, discard the marinade, and pat the meat dry with paper towels. In a medium bowl, combine the brown sugar, chili powder, dry mustard, onion powder, garlic powder, remaining 2 tablespoons salt, pepper, and cayenne and stir thoroughly. Apply this rub all over the meat. Place the roast in a large heavy roasting pan, fat-side down, and roast uncovered until the pork reaches an internal temperature of 195°F, 4 to 4½ hours. Remove the pork from the oven, cover with aluminum foil, and let rest for at least 30 minutes or as long as 1 hour (it will continue to cook as it rests, raising the internal temperature to 205°F). Pull the pork, chop it, or slice it as you wish and serve immediately on an onion roll or other bun with your favorite barbecue sauce on the side.

SLOW-COOKER BALSAMIC-GLAZED SHORT RIBS

I love to offer tips to cooks looking to save time and money, but sometimes the best advice I can give is when to splurge. The best balsamic vinegars are made with white trebbiano grape juice in Modena, Italy; they are aged like wine, are very dark in color, and have an almost syrupy texture. The expensive stuff often is aged for years and has a distinctive sweetness combined with its acidity. A little goes a long way, so splurge on a nice bottle.

Serves 8

- 5 pounds boneless beef short ribs (8 large ribs or 12 small ribs), fat trimmed
- 1 tablespoon extra-virgin olive oil
  Coarse salt and freshly ground pepper
- 3 garlic cloves, minced
- ¾ cup dry red wine
- ½ cup balsamic vinegar
- 2 sprigs fresh rosemary

1. Wash the short ribs and pat them dry with paper towels. Let them come to room temperature for 15 minutes.

2. Heat the oil in a large heavy skillet over medium-high heat. Working in batches, carefully transfer the ribs to the skillet, taking care not to overcrowd the pan, and brown the ribs on all sides, 5 to 6 minutes total. As the ribs are browned, transfer them to the slow cooker. Repeat until all the ribs are browned. When all the ribs are in the slow cooker, season them with salt and pepper.

3. Discard all but 1 tablespoon of the fat remaining in the skillet. Over medium heat, add the garlic and cook until softened, about 1 minute. Add the wine and vinegar and bring to a simmer, using a wooden spoon to scrape any browned bits from the bottom. Cook at a low simmer, whisking constantly, until the liquid is thickened, about 4 minutes.

4. Pour the liquid over the ribs in the slow cooker and add the rosemary. Cook the ribs on the low setting until the ribs are fork-tender, about 4 hours. Transfer the ribs to a platter and cover with foil to rest.

5. Skim the fat from the remaining liquid in the cooker, then pour the degreased juices into a medium saucepan and cook over medium heat until reduced and thickened, about 5 minutes.

6. Spoon the sauce over the ribs and serve immediately.

Slow-Cooker Lamb Shanks

Lamb shanks are ideal for the slow cooker treatment because they're a tough, sinewy cut, but after braising gently for a long time they become soft and succulent and falling off the bone. Serve these atop buttered egg noodles, creamy polenta, or mashed potatoes, if you like.

Serves 8

- 1 cup dry red wine
- 2 heaping tablespoons Dijon mustard
- 2 teaspoons coarse salt, plus more to taste
- 1 teaspoon freshly ground pepper, plus more to taste
- 6 to 8 bone-in lamb shanks (about 7 pounds)
- 2 medium yellow onions, coarsely chopped (about 1½ cups)
- 1 large carrot, peeled and cut into ¼-inch rounds (about ¾ cup)
- 1 large head garlic, cloves crushed
- 2 heaping tablespoons coarsely chopped fresh rosemary or 2 teaspoons dried

  Finely grated zest of 1 large lemon

1. In a medium nonreactive bowl, whisk together the wine, mustard, salt, and pepper, then pour into the insert of a slow cooker.

2. Layer the lamb shanks into the insert so they fit snugly. Scatter the onions, carrot, garlic, rosemary, and lemon zest on top. Cook the lamb on the high setting for 4 hours.

3. Stir the lamb mixture, rearranging the lamb shanks so that those closest to the bottom of the cooker are now on top. Reduce the temperature to the low setting and cook until the lamb is fork-tender, about 2 hours more. Transfer the lamb to a platter and cover loosely with foil to keep warm.

4. Using a slotted spoon, strain the vegetables from the cooking liquid and discard. Skim the fat from the cooking liquid. Season with salt and pepper. Bring the cooking liquid to a boil over high heat and cook until the liquid is thickened and reduced by half, 15 to 20 minutes. Pour the reduced pan juices over the shanks and serve immediately.

RACK OF LAMB

From the kitchen of Catherine Wallace

This is our daughter Catherine Wallace's favorite recipe, which she taught me to prepare over a decade ago; it was inspired by a French classic, Carré d'Agneau, first popularized in this country by Julia Child. The tangy mustard sauce balances the richness of the lamb and is so good you won't even miss the traditional mint accompaniment. The only thing Catherine and I disagree on is the soy sauce in this recipe. I love the flavor it adds, but Catherine believes it makes the sauce too thin. I'm leaving it in, but you may omit it if you like.

Serves 8

FOR THE SAUCE

- 8 garlic cloves
- 2 teaspoons coarse salt
- ½ cup Dijon mustard
- ¼ cup soy sauce
- 2 tablespoons dried rosemary
- 1 tablespoon lemon juice
- 1 cup extra-virgin olive oil

FOR THE LAMB

- Four 1½-pound racks of lamb, trimmed of all but a ¼-inch layer fat and frenched (each rack should have 8 ribs)
- 1 cup plain dried bread crumbs
- 8 tablespoons (1 stick) unsalted butter, melted

1. **TO MAKE THE SAUCE:** In a food processor or blender, blend the garlic with the salt to combine. Add the mustard, soy sauce, rosemary, and lemon juice and pulse a few times until smooth. With the machine running on low, gradually pour in the oil. The sauce should be the consistency of mayonnaise. Set aside.

2. **TO MAKE THE LAMB:** Preheat the oven to 500°F.

3. Wash the racks of lamb and pat them dry thoroughly with paper towels. Lay the racks on a baking sheet, or two if needed. Wrap the bones with aluminum foil to cover. Using a sharp knife, cut across the top of the racks, not too deeply, making shallow crisscross marks. Then, using a pastry brush, paint the top of the racks with the prepared mustard sauce.

4. Roast the racks for 10 minutes. Remove them from the oven and reduce the heat to 400°F. Sprinkle both sides of the racks with the bread crumbs and drizzle with the melted butter. Roast the racks for another 20 to 25 minutes or until a thermometer inserted into center registers 125°F for rare.

5. Transfer the racks to a cutting board to rest for 10 minutes. Carve into individual chops, arrange on a warmed platter, and serve.

Brisket Braised with Cranberry and Tomato Sauce

From the kitchen of Liz Dubin

It is an honor for me to share my dear friend Liz's family brisket with you. I love the sweet-and-sour balance of the cranberries with the tomatoes. At her gatherings, Liz serves her brisket sliced, then piled on a large platter with the sauce on the side in a gravy boat. Serve it with savory purple cabbage and spaetzle, if you like. A bonus of making this recipe is all the wonderful sauce it generates, which you can freeze and then make into another meal simply by using it to top spaghetti or another favorite pasta, and voilà: Instant dinner on a busy weeknight!

Serves 8

One 5-pound brisket with a 1-inch layer of fat on top

½ cup Dijon mustard

1 tablespoon Worcestershire sauce

3 tablespoons garlic paste

2 tablespoons coarse salt

1 tablespoon freshly ground pepper

½ teaspoon cayenne pepper

3 large red or yellow onions, sliced ½ inch thick (about 5 cups)

Two 29-ounce cans Hunt's tomato sauce

One 12-ounce jar chili sauce

Two 14-ounce cans whole cranberries

Two 14-ounce cans jellied cranberries

2 large red bell peppers, very finely chopped (about 3 cups)

4 large tomatoes, very finely chopped or one 28-ounce can diced tomatoes, with their juices

8 medium Idaho potatoes, scrubbed and halved

8 large carrots, peeled and cut into ⅓-inch-thick rounds (about 4 cups)

1. Wash the brisket and pat dry using paper towels and allow it to come to room temperature for 30 minutes on a large plastic cutting board.

2. Preheat the oven to 400°F and position the oven rack in the lower portion of the oven.

3. In a small bowl, combine the mustard, Worcestershire sauce, garlic paste, salt, pepper, and cayenne, stirring to combine well. Rub the seasoning paste all over and under the meat.

4. Place the onion slices in the bottom of a large roasting pan to cover and make a bed for the brisket; place the brisket on top of the onions. Pour the tomato sauce, chili sauce, whole cranberries, and jellied cranberries over the meat. Add the bell peppers and tomatoes and stir to combine well. Make sure the meat is totally covered in the sauce mixture and if needed add enough water to keep the meat submerged at all times. Transfer the roasting pan to the oven and cook for 30 minutes. Reduce the heat to 375°F and cook until the meat is tender and falling apart, 3 to 3½ hours longer. About 1 hour before the meat is done, add the potatoes and carrots to the roasting pan.

5. Once the meat and vegetables are tender, remove the roasting pan from the oven and place the brisket on a large cutting board. Stir the sauce in the pan until well mixed and then pour into a gravy boat to serve at the table. Slice the brisket into 1-inch pieces (remove the fat layer at the top), and arrange on a large platter. Place the potatoes and carrots around the meat on the platter and pour a little of the sauce over the meat to keep it moist.

Brisket Braised with Savory Fruits

From the kitchen of the Muss family

Josh Muss and his family are such close friends that I was thrilled when he shared his mom's brisket recipe with me. What makes it unique is the use of both coffee and rye bread, which add subtle flavoring and balance out the dried apricots and prunes. This brisket makes for excellent leftover sandwiches topped with a simple slaw.

Serves 8

One 5-pound flat-cut beef brisket

- 1 large onion, sliced into ¼-inch rings (about ¾ cup)
- 1 tablespoon extra-virgin olive oil
  Coarse salt
- 1 slice rye bread, torn into small pieces
- 1 cup black coffee
- ½ cup red wine
- ¼ cup chili sauce
- 8 whole peppercorns
- 1 bay leaf
- 3 whole cloves
- 3 pounds medium russet potatoes, peeled and cut into 1½-inch cubes (about 8 to 10 small potatoes or 3 to 4 large ones)
- 3 medium carrots, peeled and sliced into 1-inch rounds (about 1½ cups)
- ⅔ cup pitted prunes, quartered (about 4 ounces)
- ⅔ cup dried apricots, quartered (about 4 ounces)

1. Preheat the broiler to high. Wash the brisket and pat it dry with paper towels. In a roasting pan just large enough to hold the brisket, place the onion slices in a layer. Rub the brisket on all sides with the oil and season with the salt. Place the brisket on top of the onions. Place the pan under the broiler and broil until well browned on both sides, 8 to 10 minutes per side. Remove from the oven. Reduce the oven temperature to 325°F.

2. While the brisket is browning, in a large saucepan combine the bread with the coffee, wine, chili sauce, peppercorns, bay leaf, and cloves, and bring the mixture to a boil. When the mixture comes to a boil, remove the pan from the heat. Pour the mixture over the browned meat then cover the pan tightly with foil. Return the pan to the oven.

3. After 2½ hours, add the potatoes, carrots, prunes, and apricots to the pan, scattering them around the meat. Cover and continue cooking until the meat is fork-tender, 1 to 1½ hours more, checking every 30 minutes to ensure that the carrots aren't becoming overcooked.

4. Transfer the brisket to a cutting board and cover to rest. Using a slotted spoon, transfer the potatoes, carrots, and apricots to a bowl, cover, and set aside. Set aside the prunes, about ½ cup of the onions, and any remaining scraps of rye bread. Let the juices remaining in the pan stand for 15 minutes, then skim the fat from the top.

5. Take the prunes, onions, and rye bread and puree them in a food processor. Slowly pour in the degreased pan juices and process until smooth. Transfer the gravy to a medium saucepan to heat and, if it is too thin, simmer until reduced.

6. Thinly slice the brisket against the grain. Arrange the slices on a platter with the vegetables and any remaining prunes and apricots. Drizzle with a little gravy. Serve immediately with the remaining gravy on the side.

Casseroles and Savory Pies and Tarts

If you hear the word "casserole" and an image of leftovers held together by canned soup comes to mind, I want you to banish the thought. I encourage all home cooks to be practical thinkers, and practicality is the great advantage of the casserole: Casseroles are great for feeding crowds and they offer the built-in convenience of a one-dish meal that is almost always freezer friendly. They're also budget friendly. The only thing remaining is making them delicious, which is easy to do!

When we don't relegate casseroles to ingredients that have lived in our pantries and freezers for years and instead opt for making them with fresh and locally sourced foods, we have a modern twist on our moms' traditions. Comforting, tasty casseroles have been a mainstay in my kitchen for years; they're my go-to solution for weeknight suppers, and I like them for casual parties, too, because I can pop them in the oven and then enjoy the company of family and friends. When our whole family gathers for Soup Sunday, I skip making sandwiches for the gang and refer to several of my savory tart recipes instead. They offer warm, homemade, and tasty ways to feed our crowd.

Most of these recipes have short ingredient lists with easy-to-source items, so with a well-stocked pantry you can put together a delightful supper without needing to make an extra trip to the market.

I know some folks struggle with piecrusts, and I want to demystify that: A good store-bought selection works very well indeed. If you want to perfect a homemade version, I'm offering you some very easy methods. The bonus of making a piecrust from scratch is that you can prepare it several days prior to use and store it in the fridge until you're ready to bake.

I am here to give casseroles a good name. I know that after you try my versions you'll be on the bandwagon, too!

Baked Sausage and Peppers on a Bed of Polenta

This savory Italian dish is one that I like to prepare on busy weeknights when I know my boys are coming to dinner and I am running behind with my schedule. If you do not have time to make the polenta from scratch, just purchase tubes of prepared polenta, cut them into thick rounds, and place the slices in the bottom of the casserole dish.

Serves 8

Nonstick cooking spray

3 cups water

1½ teaspoons coarse salt, plus more to taste

2 cups instant polenta

¼ cup extra-virgin olive oil

2 pounds sweet Italian sausages (about 5 large links)

4 medium yellow, green, and/or red bell peppers, cut into ½-inch strips (about 4 cups)

1 large white onion, cut into ½-inch slices (about ¾ cup)

1 tablespoon dried Italian seasoning

Freshly ground pepper

One 32-ounce jar marinara sauce

½ cup grated Parmesan cheese

1. Preheat the oven to 350°F.

2. Lightly spray a 13 × 9-inch baking dish with nonstick cooking spray. In a medium saucepan, bring the water to a boil. Add the salt and then slowly whisk in the polenta. Cook over low heat, whisking constantly, until the polenta is thick, about 5 minutes. Pour the hot polenta into the baking dish and cover the surface directly with plastic wrap. Let stand until firm, about 20 minutes.

3. Meanwhile, heat the oil in a large heavy skillet over medium-high heat. Add the sausage links and brown on all sides, about 5 minutes total. Transfer the sausages to a plate and cover with foil to keep warm.

4. Reduce the heat to medium. Add the bell peppers and onion to the skillet and cook, stirring occasionally, until the vegetables are soft and golden, about 15 minutes. Add the Italian seasoning and season with salt and pepper, stirring to combine. Stir in the marinara sauce and continue to cook until warmed through, 5 to 7 minutes.

5. Slice the sausages into 1-inch-thick rounds and transfer them to the warm sauce. Gently pour the sausage and sauce mixture over the prepared polenta, spreading to cover the entire dish. Sprinkle the top of the casserole with the cheese. Bake until the casserole is hot and bubbling, 20 to 25 minutes.

6. Serve in warmed large wide-rimmed bowls alongside A Simple Green Salad (page 14) and garlic bread, if you like.

BAKED SPAGHETTI

You can make this up to two days in advance. To make it more decadent, top it with an additional layer of cheese and broil for the last two minutes for a cheesy crust. Alternatively, you can make it healthier by adding more vegetables to the sauce, such as chopped carrots, zucchini, fennel, and artichoke hearts. You could also make it more substantial by adding cannellini beans. For a shortcut, you can substitute four cups of jarred marinara for the homemade sauce.

Serves 8

- 2 cups canned diced tomatoes, with their juices
- 2 cups tomato sauce
- ½ cup chicken broth, homemade or store-bought
- 1 small yellow onion, diced (about ½ cup)
- 1 small green bell pepper, diced (about ½ cup)
- 2 garlic cloves, minced
- ½ cup chopped fresh flat-leaf parsley or 2 tablespoons dried
- 1½ teaspoons dried oregano
- 1½ teaspoons sugar
- ¼ teaspoon coarse salt
- ¼ teaspoon freshly ground pepper
- 2 bay leaves
- 1 pound ground turkey
- ½ pound ground pork
- 1 pound spaghetti
- Nonstick cooking spray
- 1 cup shredded mozzarella cheese
- 1 cup grated Parmesan cheese

1. In a large, heavy stockpot, combine the tomatoes with their juices, tomato sauce, broth, onions, bell peppers, garlic, parsley, oregano, sugar, salt, pepper, and bay leaves and bring to a boil over medium-high heat. Reduce the heat to medium-low and simmer, covered, for 1 hour.

2. In a large heavy skillet over moderately high heat, combine the turkey and pork and cook, stirring frequently, until thoroughly browned, about 10 minutes. Drain off the accumulated fat and pour the meat into the stockpot with the simmering sauce. Remove the bay leaves.

3. Preheat the oven to 350°F.

4. Cook the pasta to al dente according to package directions.

5. Coat a 13 × 9-inch casserole dish with nonstick cooking spray. Spread one-third of the meat sauce over the bottom of the dish. Top with half of the spaghetti. Scatter half of the cheeses over the spaghetti. Repeat the layers, ending with a last layer of sauce.

6. Bake the spaghetti until bubbling and golden brown on top, 25 to 30 minutes. Remove the baked spaghetti from the oven, cover loosely with foil, and let rest for 15 minutes. Cut the spaghetti into squares and serve on warmed plates.

CHICKEN POT PIE

I like to take the meat from a leftover roasted chicken and clean out my pantry and refrigerator to make this new dish. If you are pressed for time, use a store-bought crust. Serve with A Simple Green Salad (page 14).

Serves 8

FOR THE CRUST

2 cups all-purpose flour

½ teaspoon coarse salt

12 tablespoons (1½ sticks) cold unsalted butter, cut into small pieces

3 tablespoons ice water

1 large egg yolk, lightly beaten

FOR THE FILLING

2½ pounds boneless, skinless chicken thighs, or 5 cups cooked rotisserie chicken, shredded or cubed

Coarse salt and freshly ground pepper

5 tablespoons extra-virgin olive oil

8 ounces button mushrooms, stemmed and quartered

1 quart (4 cups) chicken broth, homemade or store-bought

1 cup frozen peas, thawed

½ cup frozen pearl onions, thawed

4 medium carrots, peeled and sliced into ½-inch-thick rounds (about 2 cups)

4 tablespoons (½ stick) unsalted butter

½ cup all-purpose flour

½ cup dry white wine

1 cup half-and-half

1 tablespoon Dijon mustard

¼ cup chopped fresh flat-leaf parsley

Nonstick cooking spray

1. **TO MAKE THE CRUST:** In a food processor, combine the flour and salt and pulse a few times to blend. Scatter the butter pieces evenly around the bowl, and pulse until the largest pieces are the size of peas, 10 to 12 times. Drizzle the water over the mixture and pulse again, until the dough forms moist crumbs that are just beginning to clump together, about 9 pulses more. Turn the crust out onto a large piece of plastic wrap and, using clean dry hands, gather into a pile. With the heel of your hand, gently smear the dough away from you until the crumbs cohere. Shape the dough into a square, wrap tightly in the plastic wrap, and refrigerate until firm, at least 2 hours or up to 2 days.

2. Position a rack in the center of the oven and preheat the oven to 350°F.

3. **TO MAKE THE FILLING:** Rinse the chicken thighs with cold water and pat dry with paper towels. Season generously with salt and pepper. In a large Dutch oven over medium-high heat, warm 2 tablespoons of the oil until very hot. Working in two batches, brown the chicken thighs, about 4 minutes per side, adding 1 more tablespoon of the oil between batches. As the thighs finish browning, transfer them to a cutting board to rest until cool enough to handle. Cut the thighs into 1-inch pieces. (It is fine if the chicken is not cooked through at this point; it will continue to cook in the pie.) Put the cut-up chicken in a large bowl and set aside.

4. Add 1 tablespoon of the oil to the pot, add the mushrooms, and cook, without stirring, for 1 minute. Continue cooking, stirring occasionally, until browned, about 4 minutes. If the mushrooms are sticking to the pot, add a little of the broth. Transfer the mushrooms to the bowl of chicken and set aside.

5. Reduce the heat to medium and add the remaining 1 tablespoon oil. Add the peas, onions, and carrots, and cook, stirring occasionally, until the edges are brown, 8 to 9 minutes. Transfer the vegetables to the bowl with the chicken and mushrooms.

6. In the same pot over low heat, melt the butter. Add the flour and cook, whisking constantly, until the mixture is bubbling, 2 to 3 minutes. Gradually whisk in the broth, wine, and half-and-half, scraping up any browned bits from the bottom of the pan, until the sauce is smooth. Bring to a slight boil, reduce the heat to low, and return the chicken and vegetables to the pot. Season with salt and pepper and add the mustard and parsley. Partially cover the pot and simmer gently for 10 minutes, stirring occasionally. Taste and adjust the seasoning, if necessary.

7. Spray a 9-inch deep-dish pie plate with nonstick cooking spray. Pour the filling into the plate and set aside.

8. On a lightly floured surface, roll out the dough into a round large enough to cover the pie plate. Gently lay the crust over the filling. With a sharp knife, make a few slits in the top so that the steam can escape and trim off any overhanging dough. Using your fingers, crimp the edges. Transfer the pie plate to a baking sheet, brush the crust with the beaten egg yolk, and bake until golden, about 30 minutes. Serve piping hot.

MOM'S CHICKEN AND RICE CASSEROLE

From the kitchen of Vana Martin

Some recipes are so comforting and remind you so much of a loved one that you wouldn't change them for the world, no matter the ingredients. That's how I feel about my mom's chicken casserole, which is always the first meal we have together when I visit her at her home in Florida. Sometimes it's great to modernize and update an old-fashioned recipe, like I do with the tuna casserole on page 110, but sometimes it's good to let a classic remain as such.

Serves 8

- 10 to 12 boneless, skinless chicken thighs (about 1½ pounds)

  Nonstick cooking spray
- Two 10¼-ounce cans cream of mushroom soup
- Two 10¼-ounce cans cream of celery soup
- Two 6.9-ounce boxes chicken-flavored Rice-A-Roni
- 2 cups cold water
- 2 teaspoons dried parsley
- 2 packages dried onion soup mix (two 1-ounce packets)

1. Wash the chicken thighs and pat them dry with paper towels. Preheat the oven to 350°F. Lightly grease a 13 × 9-inch casserole dish.

2. In a large nonreactive bowl, combine the canned soups, Rice-A-Roni, water, and parsley. Spread the mixture evenly along the bottom of the prepared casserole. Place the chicken thighs on top of the mixture and sprinkle it all over with the onion soup mix.

3. Cover the casserole tightly with aluminum foil and bake for 2½ hours ("No peeking!" says my mom). Take care not to open the oven or lift the foil during the cooking. Serve the casserole piping hot, ladled into warmed wide bowls, if you like.

Stuffed Vegetables

Using all the abundant fresh produce from your garden or from farmer's markets in the summer can be a challenge, and these recipes are my best solutions. Feel free to substitute the sausage in the stuffed tomatoes with meaty chopped mushrooms or lean ground turkey. The most important thing for these one-dish wonders is to always remove the seeds and most of the flesh of the vegetables, which makes stuffing them so much easier.

STUFFED ZUCCHINI WITH SIRLOIN, PARMESAN, AND TOMATO SAUCE

The secret to this dish is roasting the zucchini before stuffing, which cuts down the cooking time and simultaneously adds a deep oven-baked flavor!

Serves 8

8	medium zucchini (6 to 8 inches each), stem ends removed
	Coarse salt and freshly ground pepper
½	cup extra-virgin olive oil
1	large sweet onion, minced (about 1 cup)
1½	pounds ground sirloin
6	garlic cloves, minced
2	cups grated mozzarella cheese
1	cup panko bread crumbs
½	cup finely chopped fresh basil
¾	cup grated Parmesan cheese
One	28-ounce can diced tomatoes, drained

1. Preheat the oven to 425°F.

2. Halve the zucchini lengthwise. Using a small spoon, scoop out the seeds and most of the flesh of each half, taking care to leave about ¼ inch of zucchini meat around the sides and bottom. Season the cut side of the zucchini with salt and pepper and brush with ¼ cup of the oil. Set the zucchini halves cut-side down on a rimmed baking sheet and roast until slightly softened and the edges are beginning to brown, about 8 minutes. Carefully transfer the zucchini, cut-side up, in one layer into a casserole dish.

3. In a large nonstick skillet over medium-high heat, heat 2 tablespoons of the oil. Add the onion and cook until softened, about 3 minutes. Add the beef and cook until browned, about 6 minutes, then add half of the garlic and cook until fragrant, about 30 seconds more. Move the pan off the heat and stir in the mozzarella, ½ cup of the panko, and ¼ cup of the basil. Taste and adjust the seasoning with additional salt and pepper, if needed.

4. Stuff the zucchini halves with the beef mixture. In a medium bowl, toss the remaining ½ cup panko with the Parmesan. Sprinkle the panko mixture on top of the filled zucchini. Bake the zucchini until the topping is golden, 8 to 9 minutes.

5. Meanwhile, heat the remaining 2 tablespoons oil in a medium skillet over medium-high heat. Add the remaining garlic and cook until fragrant, about 30 seconds. Add the tomatoes with their juices and cook until thickened, stirring frequently, about 8 minutes. Stir in the remaining basil and season with salt and pepper.

6. Serve the zucchini immediately, with the sauce on the side.

STUFFED PORTOBELLO CAPS

In observance of Meatless Monday, which is a great idea we've adopted, I make these herb-and-cheese filled mushroom caps. I like to serve them with a fresh tomato salad.

Serves 8

- 8 large portobello mushroom caps, washed and patted dry
- 8 teaspoons extra-virgin olive oil
- 4 garlic cloves, minced
- 6 cups loosely packed baby spinach, tough stems removed and torn
- 2 tablespoons finely chopped fresh oregano or 2 teaspoons dried
- 1 cup panko bread crumbs
- 1 cup grated Parmesan cheese
- 2 tablespoons balsamic vinegar
- 2 teaspoons dried Italian seasoning
- Coarse salt and freshly ground pepper

1. Preheat the oven to 400°F and place the rack in the upper position.

2. Remove the brown gills and tough stems from the underside of the mushrooms using a spoon. Rinse with cold water and set on a paper towel.

3. In a large skillet over medium-high heat, warm 4 teaspoons of the oil.

4. Add the mushroom caps, skin-side down, scatter the garlic in the pan, and cook until softened and fragrant, about 4 minutes.

5. Remove the caps from the pan and place them in an casserole dish.

6. Add the spinach and oregano to the garlic and cook until the spinach wilts, about 2 minutes longer. Remove the pan from the heat.

7. In a medium bowl, mix together the panko, cheese, vinegar, Italian seasoning, and the remaining 4 teaspoons oil.

8. Add the spinach mixture to the panko mixture and toss well to combine; season with salt and pepper to taste. Divide the mixture evenly among the mushroom caps.

9. Bake until the stuffing is golden brown on top, 8 to 10 minutes. Remove from the oven and serve.

STUFFED TOMATOES WITH TURKEY SAUSAGE

These stuffed tomatoes make a lovely light supper with rice pilaf or steamed couscous and A Simple Green Salad (page 14).

Serves 8

    Nonstick cooking spray
 8 large or 16 small ripe heirloom tomatoes
    Coarse salt and freshly ground pepper
 2 tablespoons extra-virgin olive oil, plus more
    for drizzling
 ½ pound button mushrooms, finely diced
    (about 2 cups)
 3 garlic cloves, minced
 1 pound turkey sausage, cut into ¼-inch dice
 ¼ teaspoon crushed red pepper flakes
 2 cups lightly toasted plain dried bread crumbs
 ¾ cup grated Parmesan cheese
 ¼ cup minced fresh flat-leaf parsley or
    1 tablespoon dried
 1 tablespoon minced fresh oregano or
    1 teaspoon dried

1. Preheat the oven to 375°F. Coat a 13 × 9-inch casserole dish with nonstick cooking spray.

2. Using a paring knife, core the tomatoes. Using a spoon, scoop out the seeds and discard them. Season the insides of the tomatoes with salt and pepper. Set the tomatoes cut-side down on two large plates to drain.

3. In a large skillet over medium-high heat, heat the oil. Add the mushrooms, season with salt and pepper, and cook until the mushrooms begin to brown, about 5 minutes. Add the garlic and cook until fragrant and softened, about 1 minute. Add the sausage and red pepper flakes and cook until the sausage is warmed through, 3 to 5 minutes. Transfer the sausage mixture to a bowl and let cool for 10 minutes.

4. Stir the bread crumbs, ½ cup of the cheese, the parsley, and oregano into the sausage mixture. Spoon the filling into the tomatoes, mounding it slightly, and gently transfer each tomato into the prepared baking dish. Sprinkle the remaining ¼ cup cheese evenly over each tomato and drizzle a little oil over each. Bake until the sides of the tomatoes are soft, the stuffing is hot throughout, and the cheese is golden, 30 to 35 minutes. Let the tomatoes stand 5 minutes before serving.

BEEF ENCHILADAS

Enchiladas are a Wallace family favorite. It took me a long time to perfect a version that satisfied my craving, though. The secret is the tomatillos in the sauce. This is an ideal potluck dish. Feel free to substitute the lean ground beef with ground turkey or with 2½ cups of cooked shredded chicken.

Serves 8

Nonstick cooking spray

2 tablespoons corn oil

2 large onions, chopped (about 1½ cups)

2 garlic cloves, minced

1 pound lean ground beef

One 15-ounce can diced tomatoes, with their juices

One 4-ounce can diced green chiles, with their juices

1 cup heavy cream

2 tablespoons all-purpose flour

One 11-ounce can green tomatillos, drained

1 cup chicken broth, homemade or store-bought

2 teaspoons ground cumin

2 teaspoons chili powder

Coarse salt

Sixteen 6-inch flour tortillas

1 cup shredded Monterey Jack or pepper Jack cheese

1. Preheat the oven to 350°F. Coat a 13 × 9-inch baking dish with nonstick cooking spray.

2. Heat the oil in a large nonstick skillet over medium-high heat. Add the onion and cook, stirring occasionally, until tender, about 5 minutes. Add the garlic and cook for 1 minute more. Add the beef and brown, 3 to 4 minutes. Stir in the tomatoes and chiles and their juices. Reduce the heat and simmer until the liquid has evaporated by half, about 8 minutes. Remove from the heat and set aside to cool.

3. In a small saucepan over medium-high heat, combine the cream and flour and cook, whisking constantly, until the mixture begins to thicken, about 5 minutes. Stir in the tomatillos, broth, cumin, and chili powder and season with salt. Bring to a boil. Reduce the heat to a simmer, and cook until thickened, about 20 minutes. Set the mixture aside to cool, then thoroughly puree in a blender.

4. One by one, spoon ½ cup of the beef mixture and 2½ tablespoons of the cheese down the center of each tortilla and roll it up. Arrange the filled tortillas in the bottom of the baking dish. Cover with the pureed tomatillo-cream mixture. Sprinkle with the remaining 1 cup cheese. Bake until the cheese is bubbling and brown, about 25 minutes. Remove from the oven and let stand for 10 minutes before serving.

CRAB IMPERIAL

This is a small but rich supper. For a more elegant presentation, mound the crab imperial into scallop shells (which you can often find at home goods stores or online) and top with a sprinkle of bread crumbs. Serve with A Simple Green Salad (page 14) and crisp French bread at the table.

Serves 8

Nonstick cooking spray

1 pound fresh lump or back fin crabmeat

2 slices firm white bread

4 tablespoons (½ stick) unsalted butter

2 tablespoons finely chopped fresh flat-leaf parsley

1 teaspoon coarse salt

1 teaspoon Old Bay seasoning

1 teaspoon freshly ground pepper

½ medium onion, finely chopped (about ¼ cup)

½ small yellow bell pepper, finely chopped (about ¼ cup)

1 large celery stalk, finely chopped (about ¼ cup)

¾ cup mayonnaise

½ teaspoon dry mustard, such as Colman's or lemon juice

Pinch of Hungarian paprika (optional)

1. Preheat the oven to 400°F and position the rack in the center of the oven.

2. Lightly coat a 12 × 8-inch gratin dish with nonstick cooking spray. Place the crabmeat in a medium bowl and set aside.

3. Tear the bread into small chunks and place them in a mini food processor. Pulse several times until reduced to coarse crumbs. Melt 2 tablespoons of the butter and then drizzle over the crumbs; pulse again until finely processed. Tip the crumbs into a small bowl and set aside. Add the parsley, salt, Old Bay, and pepper to the processor and pulse several times until coarsely chopped.

4. In a small saucepan over medium-high heat, melt the remaining 2 tablespoons butter. Add the onion, bell pepper, and celery and cook until soft, about 5 minutes. Remove from the heat and let cool slightly.

5. Add the mayonnaise and mustard to the crabmeat and mix until smooth. Add the parsley mixture and mix well.

6. Pour the crab mixture into the prepared casserole and top with the bread crumbs. You can sprinkle with a pinch of paprika if you like.

7. Bake, uncovered, until bubbling and golden brown, 15 to 20 minutes. Serve right from the gratin dish at the table or in the shells.

GRANDCHILDREN'S CASSEROLE

This recipe was introduced to our family several decades ago by my children's godmother and my friend Patty Warrender. My kids call it "baby food," but it is still requested in our household. I promise that if you make this conventional casserole not only will you get your young grandchildren to eat at a family gathering, but your big kids will eat it, too!

Serves 8

Nonstick cooking spray

2 pounds lean ground beef

Coarse salt and freshly ground pepper

One 14.5-ounce family-size box macaroni and cheese, such as Kraft or Velveeta

¾ cup ketchup or barbecue sauce

1 cup shredded cheddar cheese

1. Preheat the oven to 325°F and position the rack in the center of the oven.

2. Lightly coat a 2-quart casserole dish with nonstick cooking spray.

3. In a large skillet over medium-high heat, cook the beef until well done, about 6 minutes; season with salt and pepper. Using a colander, drain off the fat, and set the meat aside.

4. In a large pot of boiling salted water cook the macaroni according to the package directions.

5. Place the beef in the bottom of the greased casserole dish and then top with the ketchup. Add the prepared macaroni and cheese and sprinkle the shredded cheese over the top.

6. Cover and cook for 20 minutes, then uncover and continue to cook until golden, 3 to 5 minutes longer. The casserole should be a little loose, not too firm or set.

SHEPHERD'S PIE

From the kitchen of The Irish Inn at Glen Echo

I adapted this recipe from one that Christy and Libby Hughes of The Irish Inn at Glen Echo in Maryland shared with me. The establishment is soaked in history, character, and charm and is perfect year-round to visit for a pint and shepherd's pie. Go Irish!

Serves 8

FOR THE TOPPING

6 Yukon gold or russet potatoes, peeled and cut into chunks (about 3 pounds)

One 8-ounce package cream cheese, softened

1 cup heavy cream

4 tablespoons (½ stick) unsalted butter

2 teaspoons finely chopped white onion

  Coarse salt and freshly ground pepper

FOR THE FILLING

1 tablespoon extra-virgin olive oil

3 pounds lean ground beef

1 tablespoon unsalted butter

3 large carrots, peeled and diced (about 1 cup)

2 medium celery stalks, diced (about 1 cup)

1 medium onion, finely chopped (about ⅔ cup)

8 ounces button mushrooms, diced (about 2 cups)

2 tablespoons Irish whiskey (optional)

2 cups veal or beef broth, homemade or store-bought

2 cups frozen peas, thawed

  Coarse salt and freshly ground pepper

2 tablespoons dried Italian seasoning

1 tablespoon ground nutmeg

1. **TO MAKE THE TOPPING:** Place the potatoes in a large saucepan and cover by 1 inch with salted water. Slightly cover and bring to a boil over medium-high heat; reduce to a simmer and cook until the potatoes are easily pierced with the tip of a paring knife, 35 to 40 minutes. Using a large colander, drain the potatoes then place them back into the dry pot on the stovetop over low heat. Mash the potatoes, allowing all of the steam to escape before adding the other ingredients. Remove from the heat and add the cream cheese, heavy cream, butter, and minced onion, and season with salt and pepper, stirring thoroughly to mix well.

2. **TO MAKE THE FILLING:** Preheat the oven to 375°F and position the rack in the middle of the oven.

3. In a large skillet over medium-high heat, warm the oil. Add the beef and cook, stirring occasionally, until browned and no longer pink, about 10 minutes.

4. Using a large colander, drain off the fat and set the meat aside. Wipe out the skillet and add the butter. Add the carrots, celery, onion, and mushrooms and cook, stirring frequently, until soft, 6 to 8 minutes.

5. Return the beef to the skillet with the vegetables and add the whiskey, if using. Stir to combine and cook for several more minutes. Add the broth and peas and mix to combine well; cook until heated through. Season with salt and pepper. Stir in the Italian seasoning and nutmeg and cook for another minute.

6. Pour the beef filling into a 13 × 9-inch casserole dish. Drop dollops of the mashed potato topping over the filling, using a spatula to spread it to the edges and make decorative peaks. Bake until the topping is golden brown and the filling is bubbling, 25 to 30 minutes. Cut into squares and serve on warmed plates at the table.

TOMATO PIES

These two easy tomato pies fall somewhere between pizza and quiche, and are among my best hits for simple summer suppers. They're both so crowd-pleasing that you can take them to your next potluck dinner and watch them disappear as guests ask you for the recipes. And they're incredibly versatile: select a different cheese, add some savory prosciutto, lay down a layer of spinach, or switch up the crusts by swapping plain pastry for puff pastry or vice versa.

TOMATO, ROASTED ONION, AND MOZZARELLA TART

The combination of the buttery crust with the fresh ripe tomatoes and the nutty caramelized onions is what makes this supper. This would be excellent accompanied with the Celery Heart Salad (page 15).

Makes 2 tarts; serves 8

4 large ripe tomatoes, cut into ¼-inch slices
  Coarse salt
1 large sweet onion, very thinly sliced (about 2 cups)
½ cup extra-virgin olive oil
2 sheets frozen puff pastry, thawed
2 large eggs, lightly beaten
1 cup grated Parmesan cheese
1½ cups shredded mozzarella cheese
2 garlic cloves, minced
4 tablespoons torn fresh basil or 4 teaspoons dried

1. Preheat the oven to 400°F.

2. Spread the tomato slices out on several layers of paper towels. Season with salt and let drain for about 30 minutes.

3. Place the onion slices in a large bowl. Add ¼ cup of the oil and toss to coat. Scatter the onion onto a large baking sheet. Roast the onion until well browned, about 25 minutes. Remove the onion from the oven and let cool on the baking sheet on a wire rack.

4. Unfold the pastry sheets on a lightly floured surface. Roll the pastry sheet into two individual 13-inch squares. Transfer the pastry sheets onto two baking sheets. Brush the pastry for both tarts all over with the egg. To form rimmed crusts, fold over the long edges of each pastry by ½ inch, then brush again with the egg. Fold over short edges ½ inch, then brush with the egg again. Sprinkle the Parmesan evenly over the bottom of each crust (about ½ cup per tart). Poke the dough uniformly with a fork. Reserve ½ cup of the mozzarella and sprinkle the rest evenly over the bottom of each tart (about ½ cup per tart).

5. Use paper towels to gently press excess moisture from the tomatoes. Layer the tomatoes evenly over the cheese. Spoon the roasted onions around the tomatoes on each tart. In a small bowl, whisk together the remaining ¼ cup oil and the garlic and drizzle over the tomatoes on both tarts. Sprinkle with the remaining mozzarella, about ¼ cup per tart.

6. Bake until the tart crusts are deep golden, 10 to 15 minutes.

7. Remove the tarts from the oven. Transfer them from the sheets to wire racks and cool for 5 minutes and then garnish with the basil. Slide the tarts onto a large cutting board, slice into pieces, and serve.

TOMATO PIE FOR SUMMER

This makes for a light supper with lots of tangy flavors thanks to the combination of Dijon mustard, basil, and Swiss cheese. It's quite rich, so each person only needs a small slice, served alongside a green salad sprinkled with whichever fresh herbs you happen to have on hand.

Makes 1 pie, serves 8

FOR THE CRUST

- 1 cup plus 2 tablespoons all-purpose flour
- 1 teaspoon sugar
- 1 teaspoon salt
- 6 tablespoons (¾ stick) cold unsalted butter, cut into ½-inch pieces
- 3 tablespoons ice water

FOR THE PIE

- 1 tablespoon Dijon mustard
- 3 large tomatoes, cut into ¼-inch slices
- 1¾ cups shredded Swiss cheese
- ½ cup loosely packed basil leaves
- Coarse salt and freshly ground pepper

1. **TO MAKE THE CRUST:** In a food processor, blend the flour with the sugar and salt. Add the butter and pulse until the mixture resembles coarse meal. Drizzle in the ice water and pulse until the dough forms small pea-size pieces. Turn the dough onto a lightly floured work surface and press it out with the heel of your hand. Gather the dough together and flatten it into a disk about 4 inches in diameter. Wrap in plastic wrap and refrigerate for at least 1 hour.

2. On a lightly floured surface, roll out the dough to a 12-inch round. Transfer to a 9-inch glass pie plate. Trim any overhanging dough and flute the edges. Prick the bottom of the shell all over with a fork and freeze until firm, about 20 minutes.

3. Preheat the oven to 450°F. Line the frozen pie shell with foil and fill with pie weights or dried beans.

4. Bake the pie until the edges are slightly golden, 20 to 25 minutes. Remove the foil and bake until the center loses its raw look, 5 to 8 minutes more. The shell should be a little light; it will be baked again. Let cool on a rack before adding the filling.

5. **TO MAKE THE PIE:** Preheat the oven to 425°F.

6. Spread the bottom of the crust liberally with the Dijon mustard. Add a layer of about half the tomato slices and then about half of the cheese. Scatter all of the basil on top and season with salt and pepper. Repeat the tomato and cheese layers.

7. Bake the tomato pie until the cheese is melted and golden, 25 to 30 minutes. Serve warm.

STUFFED SHELLS

When our family gathers for the Christmas holidays this is my go-to supper. It's a make-in-advance, tailor-to-your-taste, and feed-a-crowd kind of dish! Play with the filling for the shells anyway you prefer, adding whichever favorite ingredients you like and taking out ones you don't. The shells themselves are a smart supper idea since they can go straight from the freezer to the oven and then to the table.

Serves 8

One 12-ounce box jumbo pasta shells

2 tablespoons extra-virgin olive oil, plus more for drizzling

6 ounces thinly-sliced prosciutto, finely chopped

1 medium red onion, finely chopped (about ⅔ cup)

3 garlic cloves, minced

1½ pounds frozen spinach, thawed and well drained

1 tablespoon red wine vinegar

1 cup mascarpone cheese (8 ounces)

1 cup ricotta cheese (8 ounces)

Coarse salt and freshly ground pepper

5 cups favorite tomato sauce, homemade or store-bought

3 tablespoons cold unsalted butter, cut into small cubes

1 cup shredded mozzarella cheese

1 cup grated Parmesan cheese

1. Bring a large, heavy pot of water to boil over medium-high heat. Cook the pasta shells according to package directions. Drain the shells in a colander and rinse in cool water. Transfer the shells to a medium bowl and drizzle with a little oil to coat, then set aside to cool.

2. Heat the oil in a large, deep skillet over medium-high heat. Cook the prosciutto with the onion and garlic, stirring frequently, until the prosciutto begins to brown, 6 to 8 minutes.

3. Add the spinach to the skillet and continue cooking, stirring occasionally, until the spinach is tender but not watery, about 4 minutes.

4. Stir in the vinegar and cook until it evaporates, about 2 minutes, then remove the pan from the heat and let cool slightly, about 5 minutes. Stir in the mascarpone and ricotta, then season to taste with salt and pepper.

5. Place a rack in the center of the oven and preheat it to 375°F.

6. Pour 2 cups of the tomato sauce into the bottom of a 15 × 10-inch casserole dish.

7. Gently stuff each shell with 1 heaping tablespoon of the filling. Pack the shells side by side atop the tomato sauce in the prepared pan. You should have 32 to 40 shells in the pan. Dot each shell with a cube of butter. Cover the pan tightly with aluminum foil and bake for about 40 minutes or until the shells are warmed through. Remove the pan from the oven. Increase the oven temperature to 450°F. Scatter the mozzarella over the shells. Bake the casserole until the shells are golden and bubbly, about 15 minutes. Remove the pan from the oven, scatter with the Parmesan, and bake until golden brown, about 2 minutes more. Remove the casserole from the oven and let rest for 5 minutes.

8. Meanwhile, heat the remaining tomato sauce in a medium saucepan over medium heat until warmed. Serve the shells with the additional sauce on the side.

TACO PIE

Mexican flavors are a favorite with any crowd and especially with our grandchildren. If you prefer you can substitute the flour tortillas here with corn tortillas, which are gluten-free and add more grains to your diet. And of course you can replace the ground beef with lean ground turkey. I like to serve this savory pie with slices of fresh lime and a black bean salad to complete the supper.

Makes two 9-inch taco pies; serves 8

- 3 pounds ground sirloin
- 2 small yellow onions, minced (about ¾ cup)
- 2 garlic cloves, minced
- 2 tablespoons unsalted butter
- ¼ cup all-purpose flour
- 2 cups beef broth, homemade or store-bought
- ¼ cup taco seasoning mix
- Two 8-ounce cans plain tomato sauce
- Nonstick cooking spray
- Eight 8-inch flour tortillas
- 1 cup shredded pepper Jack cheese

1. Position a rack in the upper third of the oven and preheat the oven to 400°F.

2. In a large nonstick skillet over medium-high heat, cook the beef and onion together, stirring to break the meat apart, until the meat is browned, about 6 minutes. Add the garlic and cook until fragrant, about 1 minute. Remove the pan from the heat and set aside.

3. In a medium saucepan over medium-high heat, melt the butter. Add the flour and stir constantly to combine, about 1 minute. Gradually whisk in the broth, sprinkle in the taco seasoning, and, whisking constantly, add the tomato sauce. Bring the mixture to a boil, stirring occasionally. Stir half of the tomato sauce mixture into the pan with the beef; set aside the rest.

4. Coat two 9-inch pie plates with nonstick cooking spray. Place one tortilla in the center of each plate; top each with 1 cup of the beef mixture. Repeat the layers in each pan, ending with a tortilla on each stack. Divide the reserved tomato sauce evenly and spread half on top of each tortilla stack. Divide the cheese evenly and sprinkle on top of the tortilla pies.

5. Bake the tortilla pies until the cheese melts and begins to bubble, 15 to 20 minutes. Cool the pies slightly, about 5 minutes, then cut each pie into 4 wedges and serve.

TURKEY TETRAZZINI

Looking for what to do with your leftover Thanksgiving turkey? Cube it, load it with mushrooms, and make this creamy, comforting one-dish meal. Beyond Thanksgiving, you can substitute cooked rotisserie chicken if you like.

Serves 8

- 4 tablespoons (½ stick) plus 1 teaspoon unsalted butter, plus more for greasing the dish
- 1 pound elbow macaroni
- 1½ pounds button mushrooms, sliced (about 6 cups)
- 2 tablespoons dry white wine
- 3 cups whole milk
- ½ cup all-purpose flour
- 2 large eggs, lightly beaten
- 4 cups shredded or cubed cooked turkey
- 1 teaspoon coarse salt
  Freshly ground pepper
- ½ cup grated Parmesan cheese

1. Position a rack in the center of the oven and preheat the oven to 350°F. Grease a 13 × 9-inch casserole dish with butter and set aside.

2. In a large pot of boiling salted water, cook the macaroni according to package directions. Drain and set aside.

3. Heat the 1 teaspoon butter in a large pan over medium heat. Add the mushrooms and the wine and cook until the liquid has evaporated, about 7 minutes. Remove from the heat.

4. In a medium saucepan over medium-low heat, warm the milk until just hot and the first bubble forms on the surface; do not let boil. Remove from the heat. Heat the remaining 4 tablespoons butter in a large saucepan over medium heat, add the flour, and cook, whisking, until the roux is golden and bubbling, about 2 minutes. Gradually stir in the hot milk and cook, stirring constantly, until the sauce is smooth and thickened, about 10 minutes. Remove the sauce from the heat and once partially cooled, stir in the beaten eggs. Divide the sauce between the macaroni and the cooked turkey.

5. Add the macaroni to the prepared casserole dish, then mix in the mushrooms. Make a large well in the middle of the pasta and add the sauced turkey. Season with the salt and pepper and sprinkle with the cheese to cover. Bake until the top is golden and the casserole is heated through, 20 to 30 minutes. Serve at the table in large warmed plates.

NOT YOUR MOM'S TUNA CASSEROLE

It is surprisingly easy to update this classic casserole by replacing the high-fat and salt-laden condensed soup it is so often made with (probably known as the version you grew up eating). And if you want to eat fewer noodles, simply add more vegetables, like broccoli, to the casserole. This can be assembled without the bread crumb topping, covered tightly with plastic wrap, and refrigerated for up to 1 day before baking. Just be sure to bring the dish to room temperature before baking, and to wait to top the casserole with the panko crumbs until ready to bake.

Serves 8

Nonstick cooking spray

One 12-ounce bag egg noodles

One 16-ounce can oil-packed tuna

One 10-ounce package frozen peas, thawed and drained

3 cups shredded sharp cheddar cheese

1 tablespoon unsalted butter

1 small onion, finely chopped (about ½ cup)

1 large celery stalk, finely diced (about ½ cup)

Coarse salt and freshly ground pepper

½ teaspoon dried thyme

8 ounces baby bella mushrooms, quartered

1½ tablespoons Worcestershire sauce

¼ cup all-purpose flour

1½ cups chicken broth, homemade or store-bought

2 cups whole milk

1½ cups panko bread crumbs

1 tablespoon extra-virgin olive oil

1. Preheat the oven to 350°F and position the oven rack in the middle position.

2. Coat a 13 × 9-inch casserole dish with nonstick cooking spray.

3. Cook the noodles in salted water until al dente according to the package directions. Drain and rinse the noodles under cool water to stop them from cooking. Once cooled, pour the noodles into a large bowl and add the tuna, peas, and 2 cups of the cheese. Toss to combine.

4. In a large skillet over medium-high heat, warm the butter. Add the onion and celery and cook until softened, about 3 minutes. Season with salt and pepper, add the thyme, and continue to cook until the onion and celery are translucent, about 2 minutes longer. Add the mushrooms, reduce the heat to medium and cook until the vegetables are tender and the mushrooms' juices have evaporated, about 5 minutes longer. Add the Worcestershire sauce and stir it in, then sprinkle the flour over the entire skillet and stir constantly with a wooden spoon until the flour is completely combined with the vegetables and there are no lumps. Add the broth and stir to scrape up any brown bits. Slowly pour in the milk, stirring constantly to combine. Bring the mixture to a boil, stirring frequently. Reduce the heat to a simmer and cook, stirring, until the liquid has thickened and reduced by about ½ cup, about 8 minutes. Taste and adjust the seasoning with salt and pepper if necessary. Pour the vegetable sauce over the noodle-tuna mixture in the bowl and stir to combine. Immediately pour into the prepared casserole dish.

5. On a large flat plate, toss the panko with the oil and the remaining 1 cup cheese. Sprinkle the mixture evenly over the casserole. Bake, uncovered, until the casserole is bubbly and the top is golden, 35 to 40 minutes. Serve piping hot.

Skillets and Stovetop Suppers

The simplest way to get dinner on the table is to pull out your trusty skillet. I love a recipe that can go from cooktop to tabletop with little fuss in between, and so I've spent a lot of time developing these ideas, which are made not only for everyday suppers but also for casual weekend entertaining.

Now, there are skillet meals and then there are skillet meals. I'm sure we can all think of the stir-fries and pasta tosses that have become all too humdrum both to prepare and for our families to eat. My skillet meals possess flavor, flair, and even potential for elegant presentation. After all, when a simple meal looks appealing to your family, you've won more than half of the battle of getting them to try new and healthier dishes. I'd also like to encourage you to raid your pantry for these skillet dishes. You can get a delicious supper on the table in no time flat by being creative with the ingredients you have handy. No lime and cilantro? Why not substitute lemon and pepper instead, if that's what you've got on hand? These dishes are made to be mixed and matched.

And the very best part of skillet dishes is the fact that you only have one pan to wash up at the meal's end, so you're guaranteed a quick cleanup and more time with your family and friends.

CHICKEN CACCIATORE FOR THE WEEKNIGHT

Back by popular demand from my cookbook Mr. Sunday's Saturday Night Chicken *is this adaptation of the chicken cacciatore ("Hunter's Chicken") served at Rao's, the Italian restaurant in East Harlem, New York, one of the most exclusive restaurants in the world. Chris and I are so lucky to have a friendship with Rao's owner, Frank Pellegrino. What I love best about Frank's recipe is that you make the whole supper on the stovetop.*

Serves 8

One 3- to 4-pound chicken, cut into 10 pieces, plus 2½ to 3 pounds bone-in chicken thighs

2 teaspoons coarse salt

2 teaspoons freshly ground pepper

2 cups all-purpose flour

¼ cup extra-virgin olive oil

3 medium yellow onions, thickly sliced (about 3 cups)

2 medium green bell peppers, cut into thin strips (about 2 cups)

2 medium carrots, peeled and diced (about 1 cup)

6 garlic cloves, finely chopped

2 cups dry red wine

Two 15-ounce cans crushed tomatoes

2 cups sliced button mushrooms

6 tablespoons finely chopped fresh flat-leaf parsley or 3 teaspoons dried

1. Rinse the chicken pieces with cold water and pat dry with paper towels. Season the pieces with the salt and pepper.

2. Place the flour in a shallow dish and dredge the chicken pieces in the flour one at a time, shaking off any excess, and then transfer the pieces to a baking sheet.

3. Heat the oil in an extra-large, heavy skillet or Dutch oven over medium-high heat. Working in batches, add the chicken pieces and brown for about 5 minutes on each side; there is no need to cook the chicken pieces through, as they will finish cooking in the sauce. Transfer the browned chicken pieces from the skillet to a large plate until all the pieces are cooked.

4. Add the onions, bell peppers, carrots, and garlic to the skillet and cook, stirring, until the onions are translucent, about 4 minutes. Add the wine and reduce the heat to a simmer. Scrape to remove all the bits of meat and vegetables from the bottom of the skillet. Raise the heat to medium-high and cook for 5 minutes more to allow some of the wine to reduce slightly.

5. Return the chicken pieces to the pot and then add the tomatoes, making sure the chicken is covered with some of the vegetables and tomatoes. Cover the skillet, reduce the heat, and simmer slowly for 40 minutes.

6. Remove the cover, add the mushrooms, and simmer for 10 to 15 minutes more. Garnish with the parsley and serve in warmed deep soup bowls, if you like.

TIP

This is very much like Osso Buco with Gremolata (page 58), in that it's a great recipe for entertaining because you can prepare it all in advance, let it come to room temperature, and then simmer it slowly until you're ready to serve it. Plus, it is better the next day anyway.

Chicken Piccata with Loads of Lemon

This recipe is a weeknight wonder! It uses simple chicken breasts and a few pantry ingredients to make a quick skillet supper. Don't worry if you have some left over. It makes for a great lunch to take to work the next day along with your favorite salad.

Serves 8

- 4 large boneless, skinless chicken breasts (about 3 to 3½ pounds)
  Coarse salt and freshly ground pepper
- 1 cup all-purpose flour
- 6 tablespoons unsalted butter
- ½ cup extra-virgin olive oil
- 1 cup chicken broth, homemade or store-bought
- ¼ cup lemon juice
- 2 tablespoons drained capers
- 2 tablespoons finely chopped fresh flat-leaf parsley

1. Rinse the chicken breasts with cold water and pat dry with paper towels. Cut the chicken breasts in half horizontally. Using the flat side of a meat mallet, pound each piece between 2 pieces of plastic wrap to a thickness of ¼ inch. Season them with salt and pepper on both sides. Place the flour in a shallow dish and then dredge the breasts in the flour, shaking off any excess.

2. In a large, heavy skillet, melt 2 tablespoons of the butter and the oil over medium-high heat. When the foam subsides, add the chicken to the skillet and cook, turning once, until golden brown outside and white throughout, about 2 minutes per side. Transfer the breasts to a platter and cover loosely with aluminum foil to keep warm. (Work in batches if necessary.)

3. Add the broth, lemon juice, and capers to the skillet and stir, scraping up any browned bits. Return the chicken to the skillet and simmer for another 5 minutes. Transfer the chicken to a serving platter.

4. Add the remaining 4 tablespoons butter to the pan and whisk until the sauce comes together. Stir in the parsley and cook for 2 minutes to warm through. Pour the sauce over the chicken and serve immediately.

SPICY SKILLET SHRIMP

From the kitchen of Ann Free

When I was looking for a good shrimp recipe I turned to my friend Ann, who always talks about this shrimp dish she learned to make from a cook of hers named Vaida. Ann likes to entertain and this is one of her go-to dishes because it can be made ahead and left alone until it's time to eat. Now it is one of my simple go-tos, too. Thank you Ann, for sharing!

Serves 8

- 2 tablespoons extra-virgin olive oil
- 1 large sweet onion, finely chopped (about 1 cup)
- 2 medium jalapeño peppers, seeded and finely chopped (about ¼ cup)
- 4 garlic cloves, minced
- Coarse salt and freshly ground pepper
- One 28-ounce can diced tomatoes, with their juices
- One 6-ounce can tomato sauce, homemade or store-bought (about ¾ cup)
- ½ teaspoon crushed red pepper flakes
- Finely grated zest of 1 large lemon (about 2 tablespoons)
- 2½ pounds large shrimp (18 to 20 count), peeled and deveined
- 1 cup tender fresh garden peas or thawed frozen peas (optional)
- Steamed long-grain white rice (optional), for serving

1. Heat the oil in a large skillet over medium-high heat. Add the onion and cook until soft, about 3 minutes. Add the jalapeños and garlic and continue to cook for 1 minute longer. Season the vegetables with salt and pepper.

2. Add the tomatoes with their juices, tomato sauce, red pepper flakes, and lemon zest to the skillet and stir well to combine. Bring the mixture to a boil, then reduce the heat to a simmer and continue to cook until the mixture has thickened, 15 to 20 minutes.

3. Place the shrimp on top of the tomato mixture and cook until opaque and pink in color, about 8 minutes longer. If you like, stir in the peas and serve over a bed of rice.

TIP
It's easy to take Ann's spicy shrimp skillet and turn it into a quick version of a classic New Orleans–style shrimp Creole. Simply stir in a roux of butter and flour along with some sautéed tricolor peppers, then add a bay leaf, a dash of cayenne pepper, a dash of hot sauce, and a dash of Worcestershire sauce.

Chicken Thighs with Coconut Milk and Chilies

To make a complete supper of this dish, serve it in warmed large, wide-rimmed bowls over a bed of jasmine rice and with a garnish of fresh lime wedges.

Serves 8

- ½ cup unsweetened shredded coconut
- 3 pounds boneless, skinless chicken thighs (about 16)
- Coarse salt and freshly ground pepper
- ¼ cup sesame oil
- 1 medium yellow onion, coarsely chopped (about 1½ cups)
- 4 small green Thai chilies or 1 to 2 jalapeño peppers, seeded and minced (about ¼ cup)
- 6 garlic cloves, minced
- 2 tablespoons ground coriander
- 2 tablespoons ground cumin
- 1 tablespoon ground turmeric
- 4 cups coconut milk
- 2 stalks lemongrass, cut into 2-inch pieces
- ¼ cup lime juice

1. In a small skillet over medium heat, toast the coconut flakes, stirring constantly, until golden, 3 to 5 minutes. Remove from the heat and transfer the flakes to a plate to cool.

2. Wash the chicken pieces and pat them dry with paper towels. Season the chicken pieces lightly with salt and pepper.

3. Heat the oil in a large, heavy skillet over medium-high heat until it begins to smoke. Add the chicken and cook until golden brown on all sides, about 5 minutes per side. Transfer the cooked chicken to a large plate to rest.

4. Add the onion, chiles, and garlic to the skillet and cook until softened, about 4 minutes. Add the coriander, cumin, and turmeric and cook until fragrant, about 30 seconds more. Gradually add the coconut milk, scraping up any browned bits from the bottom of the pan with a spoon. Then return the chicken thighs and any accumulated juices from the plate, and add the lemongrass. Simmer, stirring occasionally, until the liquid is reduced by half and the chicken is tender, about 25 to 30 minutes. Remove the lemongrass from the broth and stir in the lime juice. Taste and adjust the seasonings with salt and pepper, if necessary. Sprinkle the toasted coconut on top of the chicken and serve it immediately.

GINGER SALMON STIR-FRY

You can have this simple nutritious meal on the table within 20 minutes from start to finish. What could be better for a hectic work night supper, all in one skillet?

Serves 8

Eight 6-ounce skinless salmon fillets

    Coarse salt and freshly ground pepper

2 tablespoons peanut oil

1 pound soba (Japanese-style) noodles or spaghetti

2 tablespoons vegetable oil

1 large red bell pepper, sliced into ¼-inch strips (about 1 cup)

8 scallions, thinly sliced

2 tablespoons peeled grated fresh ginger

½ cup water

3 tablespoons oyster sauce

3 tablespoons soy sauce

3 tablespoons rice vinegar

1 tablespoon sesame oil

¼ cup finely chopped fresh cilantro, for garnish

1. Season the salmon fillets generously with salt and pepper on both sides.

2. In a large nonstick skillet, heat the peanut oil over medium-high heat. Working in batches, cook the salmon fillets until opaque, 5 to 6 minutes per side, transferring each fillet to a plate to rest as you finish the remaining fillets.

3. Cook the noodles according to package directions.

4. While the noodles are cooking, wipe out the skillet you used to cook the salmon. Heat the vegetable oil over medium heat. Add the bell pepper, scallions, and ginger and cook, stirring, until softened, about 1 minute.

5. In a small bowl, whisk the water with the oyster sauce, soy sauce, vinegar, and sesame oil in a small bowl. Add the mixture to the skillet and bring to a simmer. Fold in the noodles.

6. Divide the noodle mixture between bowls. Place a salmon fillet atop each, flaking it gently. Garnish with the cilantro and serve immediately.

Fish Tacos with Pico and Guac

From the kitchen of Remick Smothers

Our son Remick is known among his family and friends for these simple skillet tacos. Any big game night at his apartment and he is the chef, feeding his friends. He buys store-bought salsas and does not really like the shredded cabbage, but I add it to my version because I like the crunch. He is an avid sports fisherman and uses any fresh "catch of the day" for his tacos, but if you're relying on the market for yours, go for any easy-to-flake white-fleshed fillets.

Serves 8

For the Pico de Gallo

- 8 medium ripe tomatoes, cored and finely chopped (about 4 cups)
- 2 small red onions, finely chopped (about 1⅓ cups)
- 2 cups loosely packed fresh cilantro leaves, coarsely chopped
- 1 medium jalapeño pepper, seeded and finely chopped
- 1 lime
  Coarse salt

For the Fish

- 2½ pounds boneless, skinless white fish fillets such as cod or tilapia
  Juice of 2 limes
- 1 teaspoon green Tabasco sauce
- 1 teaspoon chili powder
  Coarse salt and freshly ground pepper
- 2 tablespoons extra-virgin olive oil

For the Guacamole

- 1 small red onion, finely chopped (about ½ cup)
  Juice of 2 lemons
  Coarse salt
- 4 ripe medium avocados
- 1 large jalapeño pepper, seeded and finely chopped
- 1 small handful cilantro leaves, finely chopped
- 2 large garlic cloves, minced

For the Tacos

- 24 6-inch corn or flour tortillas
- 1 small head cabbage, thinly sliced, for serving
- 4 cups shredded Monterey Jack cheese, pepper Jack cheese, sharp cheddar cheese, Mexican cheese blend, queso fresco, or queso blanco, for serving
- 2 cups sour cream (optional), for serving
- 16 lime wedges (optional), for serving

1. **TO MAKE THE PICO DE GALLO:** In a medium nonreactive bowl, combine the tomatoes, onions, cilantro, and jalapeño. Halve the lime and squeeze the juice from each half over the tomato mixture. Season with salt and stir to combine. Cover the bowl with plastic wrap and refrigerate until ready to serve.

2. **TO PREPARE THE FISH:** Wash the fish and pat dry with paper towels. In a large nonreactive bowl, combine the fish with the lime juice, Tabasco, and chili powder. Let marinate, stirring occasionally, 8 to 10 minutes.

3. **TO MAKE THE GUACAMOLE:** To make the guacamole: In a medium bowl, douse the onion with the lemon juice and a liberal sprinkle of salt. Let stand for 10 minutes. Halve and pit the avocados. Using a spoon, scoop the flesh into a bowl and add the jalapeño, cilantro, and garlic. Mash with a fork into a fairly smooth dip. Taste and adjust the seasoning with more salt, if necessary.

4. **TO CONTINUE WITH THE FISH:** Remove the fish from the marinade and pat dry with paper towels. Season the fish with salt and pepper. In a large skillet over medium-high heat, warm the oil. Cook the fish until browned on both sides and opaque throughout, 5 to 6 minutes total. Allow the fish to rest, loosely covered with foil, for 5 minutes while you heat the tortillas.

5. **TO MAKE THE TACOS:** Toast the tortillas over a kitchen burner using tongs or wrap them in parchment-lined foil and heat in the oven for 5 minutes.

6. Set up a make-your-own taco buffet with the warmed tortillas, fish, pico de gallo, guacamole, cabbage, cheese, a large dish of sour cream, and plenty of lime wedges, if you like.

TIP

Pico de gallo may be made a day in advance, wrapped in plastic wrap, and stored overnight in the refrigerator. It will keep for 3 days, refrigerated.

INDIAN BUTTER CHICKEN

This recipe is another of my "golden oldies" that I'm bringing out from my cookbook files (it originally appeared in my book Mr. Sunday's Saturday Night Chicken). *Most of us need no reminding about how popular Indian food is today, but I want people to know how easy it is to make at home. I was inspired to learn how to make this dish after I attended a book signing for the Indian chef Sanjeev Kapoor. He is one of the faces of Indian cuisine in America, a talented cook, and a charming TV host.*

Serves 8

2	pounds boneless, skinless chicken thighs (about 12)
¼	cup extra-virgin olive oil
1	large onion, diced (about 1 cup)
2	shallots, finely minced (¼ cup)
4	tablespoons (½ stick) unsalted butter
1	tablespoon lemon juice
3	garlic cloves, minced
2	teaspoons ground ginger
2	teaspoons ground cumin
2	teaspoons chili powder
1	tablespoon garam masala
1	bay leaf
2	cups tomato puree
2	cups half-and-half
½	cup plain Greek yogurt
	Coarse salt and freshly ground pepper
¼	teaspoon cayenne pepper
	Steamed rice, for serving
¼	cup coarsely chopped fresh basil or cilantro, for serving
2	limes, quartered, for serving

1. Wash the chicken and pat dry with paper towels. Cut the chicken into bite-size pieces and set aside.

2. In a large sauté pan over medium-high heat, warm 1 tablespoon of the oil. Add the onion and shallots and cook, stirring, until soft and translucent, about 5 minutes. Stir in the butter, lemon juice, garlic, ginger, cumin, chili powder, 1 teaspoon of the garam masala, and bay leaf and cook, stirring, for about 1 minute. Stir in the tomato puree and cook for 2 minutes more. Stir in the half-and-half and the yogurt, reduce the heat to low, and simmer, stirring frequently, for 10 minutes. Do not allow the sauce to boil or it will separate.

3. While the sauce is cooking, heat a large skillet over medium-high heat and add the remaining 3 tablespoons oil.

4. Season the chicken with salt and pepper, then sprinkle with the cayenne. Add the chicken to the second skillet and cook, turning occasionally, until lightly browned, about 10 minutes. Reduce the heat and add the remaining 2 teaspoons garam masala. Stir a few spoonfuls of the sauce into the chicken mixture and simmer until heated through. Remove the bay leaf from the sauce. Serve over rice with the remaining sauce, basil, and a squeeze of lime juice, if you like.

LAMB CHOPS WITH SMASHED PEAS

This recipe for young spring lamb is quick and easy, a whole meal in one pan. All you need to finish this supper is crunchy pita chips and a side of tzatziki sauce, which is Greek yogurt fortified with diced cucumbers, garlic, and vinegar, which you can make yourself or find in just about any good supermarket.

Serves 8

12 to 16 rib lamb chops (about 6 pounds)
    Coarse salt and freshly ground pepper
2 teaspoons curry powder
¼ cup extra-virgin olive oil
1 medium leek, white and tender green parts only, finely chopped (about 1 cup)
6 cups frozen peas, thawed
2 teaspoons finely grated lemon zest
¼ cup lemon juice
1 tablespoon finely chopped fresh mint or 1 teaspoon dried
1 tablespoon finely chopped fresh basil or 1 teaspoon dried

1. Pat the lamb chops dry with paper towels and season with salt and pepper and the curry powder.

2. Heat 2 tablespoons of the oil in a large skillet over medium-high heat. Working in batches, cook the lamb chops to medium-rare, 4 to 6 minutes per side. As the chops finish cooking, transfer them to a platter and cover with aluminum foil to rest and keep warm.

3. Wipe out the skillet. Heat the remaining 2 tablespoons oil over medium-high heat, and cook the leeks until just tender, 5 to 6 minutes. Add the peas and, using a potato masher, gently smash the peas. Continue cooking until the peas are heated through, 10 to 12 minutes. Remove the skillet from the heat and stir in the lemon zest, lemon juice, mint, and basil and season to taste with salt and pepper. Serve the smashed peas with the lamb chops in large warmed pasta bowls, if you like.

FISH CAKES

Enjoyed throughout the Atlantic maritime community for centuries is some version of fish or seafood patties loaded with the fruits of the sea and then gently fried. In New England, these "cakes," as they're known, are served for breakfast, lunch, and dinner. That's because they're simple to make and easy to love: You can take whatever fish you like and have on hand, and blend it with herbs and bread crumbs. Pan-fry, give a squirt of lemon, and serve with your favorite sauce, and you've got the taste of New England in your own kitchen. I suggest sauces for each of the three fish cakes, but you can feel free to mix and match with them.

MUSTARD-SHALLOT SAUCE

Makes about 1 cup sauce

- 6 medium shallots, finely chopped (about ¾ cup)
- ½ cup dry white wine
- 1 cup heavy cream
- 3 tablespoons whole-grain mustard
- 1 teaspoon Dijon mustard
- Coarse salt and freshly ground pepper

In a medium saucepan, combine the shallots and wine and bring to a boil over medium-high heat. Reduce the heat and simmer until the wine evaporates, about 5 minutes. Add the cream and cook until reduced by half. Add the mustards and season with salt and pepper. Serve hot, spooned onto crab or fish cakes or salmon burgers.

LEMON HERB SAUCE

Makes about 1 cup sauce

- 1 cup mayonnaise
- 1 shallot, coarsely chopped (2 tablespoons)
- 2 tablespoons extra-virgin olive oil
- 2 tablespoons coarsely chopped fresh tarragon or 2 teaspoons dried
- 2 tablespoons coarsely chopped fresh flat-leaf parsley or 2 teaspoons dried
- 2 tablespoons coarsely chopped fresh dill or 2 teaspoons dried
- 2 tablespoons lemon juice
- 1 tablespoon capers, drained
- 2 oil-packed anchovy fillets, drained
- Coarse salt and freshly ground pepper

In a food processor, mix all of the ingredients except the salt and pepper until smooth. Season with salt and pepper and scrape the sauce into a bowl. Cover and refrigerate until ready to use, up to 2 days.

CLASSIC TARTAR SAUCE

Makes about 1 cup sauce

- 1 cup mayonnaise
- ¼ cup minced red onion
- ¼ cup sweet pickle relish or dill pickle relish
- ¼ cup minced fresh flat-leaf parsley
- 2 tablespoons chopped drained, rinsed capers
- 4 teaspoons lemon juice

In a small bowl, stir together the mayonnaise, onion, relish, parsley, capers, and lemon juice. Cover and refrigerate for up to 2 to 3 days.

CRAB CAKES WITH MUSTARD-SHALLOT SAUCE

The charms of crab cakes are well known, and many versions of them from homey to haute abound. I like mine with a lot of sweet crab and not a lot of bready filler. This is a classic, straight-up formula to use when you have some really good fresh crab.

Serves 8

- 2 slices firm white bread
- 4 tablespoons (½ stick) unsalted butter
- 1 large celery stalk, finely chopped (⅔ to 1 cup)
- 4 scallions, white and tender green parts only, finely chopped (about ½ cup)
- ½ cup loosely packed fresh flat-leaf parsley leaves
- Coarse salt and freshly ground pepper
- 2 pounds jumbo lump crabmeat
- 2 large eggs, beaten
- ¼ cup mayonnaise
- 2 tablespoons Dijon mustard
- 2 tablespoons Worcestershire sauce
- 2 tablespoons extra-virgin olive oil
- Mustard-Shallot Sauce (optional), for serving (page 125)
- Classic Tartar Sauce (optional), for serving (page 125)

1. Line a large baking sheet with waxed paper and set aside.

2. Tear the bread slices into small chunks and place them in a mini food processor. Pulse a few times until they become coarse crumbs. Melt 2 tablespoons of the butter. Drizzle it over the crumbs and pulse again until finely processed. Tip the crumbs into a small bowl and set aside.

3. Wipe out the mini processor. Add the celery, scallions, and parsley. Season with salt and pepper. Pulse a few times to combine. Set aside.

4. In a medium bowl, combine the crabmeat with the eggs, mayonnaise, mustard, and Worcestershire. Stir gently to combine. Pour in the vegetable-herb mixture and the bread crumbs and gently combine.

5. Use a ¾-cup dry measuring cup to scoop the crab mixture and then, using your hands, gently form loose cakes. Place each on the prepared baking sheet. Chill the cakes in the refrigerator for at least 30 minutes and up to 4 hours.

6. Heat the remaining 2 tablespoons butter with the oil until the butter just melts in a large heavy skillet over medium-high heat. Working in batches, pan-fry the crab cakes until golden brown, 3 to 4 minutes per side. Transfer to a large plate and cover loosely with foil to keep warm until all the crab cakes are finished.

7. Choose your sauce, Mustard-Shallot or Classic Tartar (page 125).

SALMON BURGERS WITH LEMON HERB SAUCE

Salmon burgers make a fun, pleasing weeknight dinner; even though "burger" is in the title, you don't feel as if you've eaten badly. I like the salmon mixture's texture to be as smooth and "burgerlike" as possible, so I process it in the food processor.

Serves 8

2½ pounds skinless salmon fillets, cut into 1-inch cubes

4 scallions, white and tender green parts only, coarsely chopped

Coarse salt and freshly ground pepper

½ cup panko bread crumbs

¼ cup Dijon mustard

2 tablespoons extra-virgin olive oil

8 hamburger buns, split and lightly toasted

Butter for hamburger buns (optional)

Lemon Herb Sauce (optional), for serving (page 125)

1 large tomato, thinly sliced

1½ cups loosely packed salad greens

1. In a food processor, combine the salmon with the scallions and season with salt and pepper. Pulse to thoroughly combine, about 30 times. Transfer the mixture to a large nonreactive bowl. Add the panko and mustard and stir gently to thoroughly combine, taking care not to overmix. Form the salmon mixture into 8 patties about ¾ inch thick. Transfer the patties to two large plates and refrigerate, loosely covered in plastic wrap, for 10 minutes.

2. In a large skillet, heat 1 tablespoon of the oil over medium-high heat until shimmering. Add 4 of the salmon patties. Cook until well browned on one side, about 3 minutes. Flip the patties, reduce the heat to medium, and cook until well browned and just cooked through, about 3 minutes longer. Transfer the patties to a large plate, cover loosely with foil, and keep warm while you repeat with the remaining 1 tablespoon oil and 4 salmon patties.

3. To serve, gently toast the hamburger buns and lightly butter them, if you like, then set a warm salmon patty on the bottom half. Top with a heaping tablespoon of Lemon Herb Sauce or your favorite sauce, if you like, a slice or two of tomato, and some salad greens. Serve immediately.

FISH CAKES

From the kitchen of Nelson Sigelman

Over a decade ago in Martha's Vineyard, my late father-in-law, Mike Wallace, introduced our family to Nelson Sigelman. Our son Remick, six years old at the time, wanted to do nothing but fly-fish for the entire vacation. Nelson is an accomplished writer and the senior editor of the Martha's Vineyard Times—*and an avid outdoorsman. When he comes by to go fishing with Remick or to just visit, he always treats us to his delicious bluefish spread and these yummy fish cakes, made with striped bass.*

Serves 8

- 3 pounds striped bass fillets, skinned
- 2 scallions, white and tender green parts only, thinly sliced (¼ cup)
- ½ cup lemon juice
- 2 shallots, minced (¼ cup)
- ¼ cup chopped fresh flat-leaf parsley
- ¼ cup mayonnaise
- 2 teaspoons Dijon mustard
- 2 teaspoons coarse salt
- Pinch of cayenne pepper
- ½ cup panko bread crumbs
- ½ cup vegetable oil
- Classic Tartar Sauce (page 125), for serving

1. Pat the fish dry with paper towels. Cut the fillets into 1-inch cubes. Working in batches, add the fish cubes to a food processor and lightly process, about 10 pulses, to coarsely but evenly chop. As you finish each batch of fish, transfer to large nonreactive bowl.

2. Stir in the scallions, lemon juice, shallots, parsley, mayonnaise, mustard, salt, cayenne, and panko, and gently mix together, taking care not to overhandle the fish. Using a ⅓-cup dry measuring cup, form 16 fish cakes. Gently transfer each one onto a large baking sheet (or two, if needed). Chill the fish cakes for at least 20 minutes or up to 1½ hours to ensure that they don't fall apart when cooked.

3. In a large, heavy skillet, heat the oil over medium-high heat. Working in batches, gently slide the fish cakes into the hot oil and cook until golden brown, about 2 minutes per side. Slide the cooked fish cakes onto a large plate and cover loosely with foil to keep warm until all of the cakes are cooked. Serve immediately with Classic Tartar Sauce or other favorite sauce.

Linguine con Vongole

From the kitchen of Nancy Ellison

This is a recipe I ask my friend Nancy to make when we get together in Martha's Vineyard each summer. At first, Chris could not believe I would invite ourselves over and make this request of my friend, but now he does the asking. Nancy says although she likes to serve the dish with the fresh clams still in their shells, she also likes throwing in a can of baby clams to enrich the sauce.

Serves 8

- 2 pounds linguine
- ½ cup extra-virgin olive oil
- 8 tablespoons (1 stick) unsalted butter
- 5 garlic cloves, slivered
- 1 medium shallot, finely chopped (about 2 tablespoons)
- ½ teaspoon crushed red pepper flakes, or according to taste
- 1½ cups dry white wine
- 1 cup bottled clam juice
- 3 pounds littleneck clams, thoroughly scrubbed and rinsed well
- One 16-ounce can baby clams
- Coarse salt and freshly ground pepper
- ½ cup finely chopped fresh oregano
- ½ cup finely chopped fresh flat-leaf parsley

1. Prepare the sauce while the pasta is cooking to ensure that the linguine will be hot and ready when the sauce is finished.

2. Bring a large pot of salted water to a boil, add a drop of oil to it, add the pasta, and cook until al dente according to package directions. Set aside 1 cup of the pasta's cooking water, then drain the pasta well and rinse with cold water.

3. Meanwhile, in a large, heavy skillet, heat the oil over medium heat. Melt 4 tablespoons of the butter into the oil. Add the garlic, shallot, and red pepper flakes and cook, stirring, until just softened and fragrant, about 2 minutes. Add the wine, clam juice, and pasta water. Bring to a simmer, then add the littleneck clams. Cover and cook, shaking the pan periodically, until all the clams have opened, about 7 minutes. Discard any that have not opened.

4. Raise the heat to medium-high. Add the drained linguine to the pan. Add the remaining 4 tablespoons butter and the canned clams and season with salt and pepper. Toss the pasta with the clams until it's coated in the pan sauce. Shower the pan with the chopped herbs and serve immediately.

NOTE

Nancy likes to use a three-tiered wooden bamboo steamer to ensure tender, soft clams, and to prepare the sauce in a wok. I simplified her method here, but you're welcome to try it her way, too.

PIZZA PORK CHOPS

Our daughter Sarah just loves anything Italian: the art, the clothes, and especially the cuisine. She will always choose an Italian restaurant for our mother-daughter nights. One evening, we ordered these simple pork chops. Sarah is such a good cook that, together, we came home and made these a Wallace Skillet Supper. I promise it will make your "Italian" food lover excited, too!

Serves 8

- 8 center-cut bone-in pork loin chops, each about 1 inch thick (about 6 pounds)

  Coarse salt and freshly ground pepper

- ¼ cup extra-virgin olive oil

- 2 medium yellow onions, thinly sliced (about 1½ cups)

- Two 15-ounce cans diced tomatoes, with their juices

- 2 teaspoons dried oregano

- 1 teaspoon dried basil

- ½ teaspoon crushed red pepper flakes

- ¼ cup fresh flat-leaf parsley leaves, finely chopped, or 1 tablespoon dried (optional), for serving

1. Wash the pork chops and pat dry with paper towels. Season the chops with salt and pepper on both sides.

2. Heat the oil in a large, heavy skillet over medium-high heat. Working in batches, add the chops to the skillet and cook until they are brown and golden, about 3 minutes per side. As they finish cooking, transfer the chops to a platter and cover with foil to rest.

3. Add the onions to the skillet and cook, stirring, until tender, 4 to 6 minutes. Add the tomatoes and their juices, the oregano, basil, and red pepper flakes. Reduce the heat and simmer until the juices thicken and the sauce reduces by about one-quarter, about 15 minutes. Taste and adjust the seasonings if needed.

4. To serve, place 1 pork chop on a warmed plate and spoon the sauce on top. Scatter with the parsley, if you like.

Rigatoni with Lamb Ragu

From the kitchen of Luigi Diotaiuti

This recipe was generously shared with me by the chef Luigi Diotaiuti, whose Italian restaurant Al Tiramisu in Washington, D.C., is one of our favorites. Chef Luigi serves this lamb ragu with homemade pappardelle pasta and it happens to be the favorite dish of his brother, Giovanni. I adapted the dish for home cooks, chiefly because it's far easier to use a readily available dried pasta like rigatoni, which is thick and can easily be coated by this rich, meaty sauce. The only thing you have to remember here is that the lamb must be marinated overnight before you can make the sauce. But as Chef Luigi says, "Le cose buone non si fanno mai in fretta"—you can't rush a good thing.

Serves 8

- 9 ounces boneless leg of lamb, shoulder, or stew meat
- 3 sprigs fresh rosemary
- 3 sprigs fresh thyme
- 3 garlic cloves, peeled
- 5 bay leaves
- 2½ cups dry red wine
- 2 tablespoons all-purpose flour
- ¼ cup extra-virgin olive oil
- 3 tablespoons diced onion
- 3 tablespoons diced carrot
- 3 tablespoons diced celery
- ⅓ cup tomato sauce, homemade or store-bought
- ½ ounce dried porcini mushrooms, soaked in 1½ cups cold water for 10 minutes, drained, and finely chopped (about 1 tablespoon)
- 1 quart (4 cups) beef stock, homemade or store-bought
- Coarse salt
- 2 pounds rigatoni
- Grated Parmesan cheese (optional), for serving

1. With a sharp knife, cut the lamb into 1-inch cubes and place in a large nonreactive bowl with the rosemary, thyme, garlic, and bay leaves. Add enough wine to just below the covering point. Stir, cover, and refrigerate overnight.

2. Drain the meat from the marinade, reserving the marinade. Pat the meat thoroughly dry with paper towels. Arrange the meat on a plate and sprinkle with the flour, turning to coat on all sides. Heat 2 tablespoons of the oil in a large saucepan over medium heat. Add the onion, carrot, and celery and stir. Cook until the vegetables are tender and slightly golden, about 5 minutes. Add the floured lamb cubes and brown evenly on all sides, 6 to 8 minutes. Once the lamb begins to stick to the bottom of the pan, add the marinade and cook until it evaporates, using a wooden spoon to scrape up any browned bits from the bottom of the pan.

Add the tomato sauce and mushrooms and stir well. Add enough stock to cover the lamb and stir to combine well. Cover and reduce the heat to medium-low. Cook for 1½ hours, carefully removing the lid and stirring every 15 minutes or so, and adding more broth as it cooks down. You should always have about ½ inch of stock covering the lamb. The sauce is ready when it is highly aromatic and thickened, yet still quite fluid. Season with salt to taste.

3. Bring a large pot of salted water to boil over high heat. Add the pasta and cook until al dente according to package directions. Drain the pasta and toss with the remaining 2 tablespoons oil.

4. Add the pasta to the lamb sauce and combine gently. Serve immediately, with the cheese, if you like.

SHRIMP SCAMPI SKILLET

You can easily dress up this super-fast meal by making it a seafood combo: Combine half the shrimp with some scallops. Chris loves orzo so that is what I serve this with, but you might prefer another kind of pasta, rice, or polenta with your shrimp.

Serves 8

- 2 tablespoons extra-virgin olive oil
- 2½ pounds large (16 to 20 count) shrimp, peeled, deveined, and tails left on
- 6 garlic cloves, minced
   Coarse salt and freshly ground pepper
- 2 scallions, white and tender green parts only, thinly sliced (¼ cup)
- 2 tablespoons finely chopped fresh flat-leaf parsley or 2 teaspoons dried
- ¼ cup lemon juice
- ¼ cup dry white wine

In a large skillet, heat the oil over medium-high heat. Add the shrimp and cook until pink on one side, about 2 minutes. Using tongs, turn the shrimp, add the garlic to the pan, and cook, stirring occasionally, until the shrimp are pink, about 2 to 3 minutes more. Season with salt and pepper to taste, stir, and quickly add the scallions, parsley, lemon juice, and wine. Stir together and serve immediately.

SHRIMP AND GRITS

Crook's Corner is a legendary temple of upscale Southern cuisine in Chapel Hill, North Carolina. It was founded in 1982 by the late chef and cookbook author Bill Neal (his cookbook Biscuits, Spoonbread, and Sweet Potato Pie *is a classic), and is helmed today by the chef Bill Smith. It is hard to pinpoint exactly which Southern restaurant was the first to serve this low-country favorite in its dining room, but a lot of folks in the region credit Crook's—and so will I. Crook's guards their recipe zealously, but here is my adaptation.*

Serves 8

FOR THE SHRIMP

- 2 pounds (16 to 20 count) fresh shrimp, peeled and deveined
- 12 slices bacon (about ¾ pound)
- 1 tablespoon peanut oil, or more if needed
- 12 ounces button mushrooms, sliced (about 4 cups)
- 1 bunch scallions, thinly sliced (about 2 cups)
- 3 garlic cloves, minced
- ¼ cup lemon juice
  Hot sauce, to taste
  Finely chopped fresh flat-leaf parsley, to taste
  Coarse salt and freshly ground pepper

FOR THE GRITS

- 8 cups water
- 2 cups stone-ground grits
  Coarse salt
- 8 tablespoons (1 stick) unsalted butter
- 2 cups grated sharp cheddar cheese
- 1 cup grated Parmesan cheese
  Pinch each of white pepper, cayenne pepper, and nutmeg

1. **TO MAKE THE SHRIMP:** Wash the shrimp and pat dry with paper towels. Dice the bacon into ½-inch pieces and cook in a large nonstick skillet over medium heat until crisp, about 10 minutes. Remove the bacon and set aside. Add enough oil, about 1 tablespoon or so, to the bacon fat in the skillet to make a thin layer. Once hot, add the shrimp. Cook, stirring, until the shrimp start to color, about 2 minutes, then add the mushrooms. Add the scallions and garlic. Stir in the lemon juice, hot sauce, parsley, and salt and pepper.

2. **TO MAKE THE GRITS:** Bring the water to a boil in a large saucepan. Slowly stir in the grits. Reduce the heat to low and simmer, stirring occasionally, until the grits are thick and tender, about 20 minutes. Season with salt and stir in the butter. Stir in the cheeses and the white pepper, cayenne, and nutmeg. Taste and adjust the seasonings if needed.

3. To serve, divide the cheese grits among eight warmed plates. Spoon the shrimp and bacon over the grits and serve immediately.

Striped Bass with Pancetta, Tomatoes, and Greens

Striped bass, or rockfish, swim the East Coast year-round. Lucky me! What's local to me is one of the most sought-after fish in the North Atlantic, prized for its texture, which is a perfect balance of meaty and flaky. These fish are best to eat when they measure between 18 and 36 inches.

Serves 8

Eight 6-ounce skin-on striped bass fillets

Coarse salt and freshly ground pepper

3 tablespoons extra-virgin olive oil

6 ounces thinly sliced pancetta, finely chopped

½ medium onion, coarsely chopped (about ½ cup)

4 garlic cloves, minced

1 teaspoon crushed red pepper flakes

4 cups ripe cherry tomatoes, halved

2 teaspoons balsamic vinegar

1 teaspoon dried Italian seasoning

4 cups loosely packed baby arugula (optional), for serving

1. Wash the fish fillets, pat dry with paper towels, and place the fillets on a large plate. Season the fish with salt and pepper on both sides.

2. Heat 2 tablespoons of the oil in a large skillet over medium-high heat. Working in batches, add the fish fillets, skin-side down, and cook until lightly browned, about 6 minutes. Flip the fish and cook until the fish is firm throughout, about 3 minutes more. As each fillet finishes cooking, transfer it to a platter and lightly cover with foil to keep warm.

3. Add the remaining 1 tablespoon oil to the skillet and, still over medium-high heat, add the pancetta and cook until it begins to brown, 4 to 6 minutes, stirring occasionally. Add the onion, garlic, and red pepper flakes and cook until the pancetta is browned and crisp and the onion is soft, about 5 minutes more. Add the tomatoes, vinegar, and Italian seasoning and cook until the tomatoes are soft, about 3 minutes longer, stirring frequently. Taste and adjust the seasoning with salt and pepper.

4. Serve the fish on top of a bed of arugula on warmed plates, if you like, topped with the sauce.

TURKEY, WHITE BEAN, AND SPINACH HASH

This is a Wallace supper staple, a quick meal-in-one-skillet that's loaded with protein and nutritious greens.

Serves 8

- ½ cup extra-virgin olive oil
- 3 garlic cloves, minced
- 3½ pounds ground turkey
- Coarse salt and freshly ground pepper
- 3 cups chicken broth, homemade or store-bought
- 4 cups canned cannellini beans, rinsed and drained
- Two 10-ounce bags fresh spinach, tough stems removed
- 2 cups fresh basil leaves, torn
- Grated Parmesan cheese (optional), for serving

1. Heat the oil in a large, heavy skillet over medium-high heat. Add the garlic and cook, stirring, until fragrant, about 1 minute. Add the turkey and season with salt and pepper. Cook, using a wooden spoon or spatula to break up the meat, until the meat is browned, 8 to 10 minutes.

2. Add the broth to the skillet and scrape up any browned bits from the bottom of the pan. Raise the heat, bring the mixture to a boil, and then reduce the heat and simmer until the liquid has reduced slightly, 10 to 12 minutes. Stir in the beans and spinach and cook until heated through, stirring, about 4 minutes.

3. Remove from the heat and stir in the basil. Serve topped with the cheese alongside a nice green salad, if you like.

Veal Paillard with Charred Tomatoes

I love a good steak salad, but it's not always practical and I don't always feel like firing up the grill. I find that slender cuts of meat like veal and lamb rib chops make an excellent and quick alternative for a meat-and-fresh greens meal. Here, the warm grape tomatoes and shaved Parmesan cheese give this a classic Italian flair.

Serves 8

- ½ cup extra-virgin olive oil
- ¼ cup apple cider vinegar
- 2 small shallots, minced (about ¼ cup)
- 2 teaspoons Dijon mustard
  Coarse salt and freshly ground pepper
- 8 rib-in veal chops, about ½ inch thick (about 6 ounces each)
- 2 tablespoons dried oregano
- 1½ pints cherry tomatoes
- 8 cups loosely packed arugula
- ½ cup plus 2 tablespoons shaved Parmesan cheese

1. In a large bowl, whisk ¼ cup of the oil together with the vinegar, shallots, and mustard. Season the vinaigrette with salt and pepper and set aside.

2. Pat the veal chops dry with paper towels and season them with the oregano and salt and pepper, rubbing the spices into the meat until evenly coated.

3. Heat a large, heavy skillet over medium-high heat and add the tomatoes. Cook, shaking the pan occasionally to disperse the tomatoes and evenly cook them, until the tomatoes are charred and their skins begin to split, 6 to 8 minutes. Add the charred tomatoes to the vinaigrette and, while stirring, lightly smash the tomatoes to release some of their juices.

4. Add the remaining ¼ cup oil to a large, heavy grill pan and heat over medium-high heat until just smoking. Working in batches, grill the chops until just cooked through, 3 to 4 minutes per side. Transfer to a platter and cover loosely with aluminum foil to keep warm and rest while you finish cooking all of the chops.

5. To serve, pile 1 cup arugula onto each plate. Top with some of the tomato vinaigrette and 1 tablespoon of the cheese. Then place a veal chop beside the salad and serve immediately.

Two-By-Two Suppers

This cookbook is full of large recipes, the kind that are meant to feed a crowd. But what happens when the crowd isn't around?

In my chicken book, I created a similar chapter with my three grown children in mind, so they could make simple meals at the end of a busy day, with enough left over for the next day's lunch. I discovered that the chapter helped some unexpected other folks: My empty-nester and live-alone friends found solutions for meals, too.

Now that Chris and I are empty-nesters, I spend a lot of time thinking about "dinner for two," and how to make it special. I also think about how I can make it less of a chore when it's just the two of us. Here are my solutions for the kind of healthy, quick, and easy dinners for two that won't drive you to call takeout. And since preparing meals for your family is an act of love, I thought it would be nice to include a romantic Valentine's Day fondue dinner for two.

CHICKEN CORDON BLEU PINWHEELS

This recipe is a French twist, made healthier by not frying the chicken but still keeping the French élan by slicing it into elegant "pinwheel" rounds. I like to serve it with either roasted broccoli or roasted asparagus, depending on the season.

Serves 2

Nonstick cooking spray

Two 6-ounce boneless, skinless chicken breasts

Coarse salt and freshly ground pepper

2 ounces sliced Swiss cheese (2 thin slices)

4 ounces sliced French ham (4 thin slices)

1 large egg, lightly beaten

¼ cup seasoned dried bread crumbs or panko bread crumbs

2 tablespoons unsalted butter, melted

1. Preheat the oven to 350°F. Coat a baking sheet with nonstick cooking spray.

2. Wash the chicken breasts in cold water and pat them dry with paper towels. Trim off any excess fat. Place each breast between 2 pieces of plastic wrap and, using the flat side of a meat mallet, pound each breast to a thickness of about ¼ inch. Place the breasts on a cutting board and season generously with the salt and pepper. Place 1 slice of the cheese and overlap 2 thin slices of the French ham on top of each breast. Roll up each breast like a jelly roll, securing with toothpicks or tying with kitchen twine.

3. Put the beaten egg in one medium bowl and the bread crumbs in another. Coat the stuffed breasts with the egg. Then add the stuffed breasts, one by one, to the bowl of bread crumbs and coat with the crumbs, gently pressing the bread crumbs onto the chicken so that they adhere. Transfer the chicken breasts to the prepared baking sheet and let stand for 15 minutes.

4. Drizzle the melted butter over the chicken and bake until the crumbs are golden and the chicken is no longer pink, 20 to 30 minutes. Remove the chicken from the oven and let it rest, loosely covered with foil, for 5 minutes. Slice each breast vertically into 3 or 4 even pieces and serve immediately.

Coquilles St. Jacques

For a special presentation, look for large scallop shells at your favorite home goods store. Then serve this classic French dish with the scallops in the shells and some sautéed spinach.

Serves 2

- 3 teaspoons extra-virgin olive oil
- 1 shallot, finely chopped (2 tablespoons)
- 1 garlic clove, minced
- ½ cup canned crushed tomatoes
- ¼ cup plus 1 tablespoon dry white wine or fish broth, homemade or store-bought
- 2 teaspoons finely chopped fresh flat-leaf parsley or ½ teaspoon dried
- 2 teaspoons finely chopped fresh basil or ½ teaspoon dried
  Coarse salt and freshly ground pepper
- 1 pound large sea scallops (8 to 10 scallops)
- 1 tablespoon plus 1 teaspoon all-purpose flour

1. In a large, heavy skillet, heat 2 teaspoons of the oil over medium-high heat. Add the shallot and cook until soft, 2 to 3 minutes. Add the garlic and cook for 1 minute longer. Add the tomatoes, wine, parsley, and basil. Season to taste with salt and pepper. Reduce the heat to medium and cook until the sauce is slightly reduced and thickened, 3 to 5 minutes. Remove the skillet from the burner and set it aside.

2. Wash the scallops and pat them dry with paper towels. Make sure the scallops are thoroughly dry so they'll brown nicely.

3. Put the flour in a shallow plate and season it with salt and pepper, then dredge the scallops, shaking off any excess.

4. In a large nonstick pan over medium-high heat, warm the remaining 1 teaspoon oil, swirling to evenly coat the pan. Cook the scallops until golden brown on each side and opaque throughout, 3 to 5 minutes total. Transfer the scallops into the tomato-wine mixture, and stir gently to coat the scallops. Serve immediately.

Lobster Pot Pies

This is a dish that seems very decadent, but because you're only buying lobster for two and using it as a filling for pot pies, it's quite reasonable. The puff pastry topping is what gives it the "wow" factor.

Serves 2

- 1 sheet frozen puff pastry, thawed but chilled
- 1½ tablespoons unsalted butter
- 1 tablespoon extra-virgin olive oil
- 3 large celery stalks, finely chopped (about ¾ cup)
- 1 small white onion, finely chopped (about ½ cup)
- Coarse salt and freshly ground pepper
- 2 tablespoons all-purpose flour
- ½ cup dry white wine
- ½ cup lobster juice, fish broth, or clam juice
- ½ cup whole milk
- 1 teaspoon finely grated lemon zest
- 1½ tablespoons lemon juice
- 1 pound fresh cooked lobster (tail and claw meat), coarsely chopped
- ¾ cup frozen peas, thawed
- 1 large egg yolk whisked with a splash of water

1. Position a rack in the center of the oven and preheat the oven to 375°F. Lightly grease two small (16-ounce) ovenproof bowls.

2. On a lightly floured surface, roll out the chilled puff pastry to ¼ to ⅛ inch thick. Using a bowl of the same size as your pot pies as a guide, use a sharp knife to cut two rounds, then carefully transfer the puff pastry rounds to a baking sheet and refrigerate them until ready to use.

3. In a large skillet, heat the butter and oil over medium-high heat until just foaming. Add the celery and onion and cook, stirring occasionally, until softened and slightly golden, about 5 minutes. Season with salt and pepper.

4. Add the flour and cook, stirring constantly, for 1 minute; do not let it become brown. Add the wine, lobster juice, milk, lemon zest, and lemon juice and simmer, whisking occasionally to combine, until the mixture is slightly thickened, about 5 minutes. Remove from the heat.

5. Stir in the lobster and peas. Taste and adjust the seasoning with more salt and pepper, if needed, and then set aside to cool slightly.

6. Divide the mixture evenly between the prepared bowls. Lay the pastry rounds on top of each bowl to fit, and, using a knife, cut 4 vents, about 1 inch long each, on the top. Brush the pastry tops with the beaten egg yolk.

7. Bake until the lobster mixture is bubbling and the pastry is golden brown, 25 to 30 minutes.

8. Remove from the oven and let cool slightly, for about 5 minutes, before serving.

MONKFISH WITH SMASHED POTATOES AND WATERCRESS

They say monkfish is "poor man's lobster." I don't know about that. I especially love monkfish's wonderful meaty flesh and the way it holds up next to the hearty potatoes and crisp watercress in this recipe. Don't have watercress on hand? You can substitute dandelion greens, spinach, kale, or any other leafy green.

Serves 2

Two 6-ounce monkfish fillets

Coarse salt and freshly ground pepper

½ pound small new potatoes (about 4 or 5)

2 tablespoons extra-virgin olive oil

½ cup watercress, thick stems removed and coarsely chopped

Finely grated lemon zest, for garnish

1. Wash the fish fillets and pat them dry with paper towels. Season them lightly with salt and pepper.

2. Position a rack in the middle of the oven. Preheat the oven to 400°F.

3. Put the potatoes into a medium pot and fill the pot with salted water. Bring to a boil over high heat. Reduce the heat to a simmer and cook the potatoes until tender when pierced with a fork, about 15 minutes.

4. While the potatoes are cooking, heat 1 tablespoon of the oil in a large ovenproof skillet over medium-high heat. Cook the fish until lightly golden on each side, 6 to 8 minutes total. Transfer the pan to the oven and roast for 10 to 12 minutes or until the fish is moist but cooked through. Remove the pan from the oven, transfer the fish to a plate and cover loosely with foil, and let the fish rest until ready to serve. Reserve the pan.

5. When the potatoes are done, drain them thoroughly in a colander and add them to the pan in which you cooked the fish. Add the remaining 1 tablespoon oil. Using the back of a wooden spoon, gently smash each potato against the side of the pan until it just bursts open. Season the potatoes with salt and pepper and stir in the remaining fish juices in the pan. Add the watercress and gently mix it in with the potatoes until well combined.

6. To serve, place half of the potato-watercress mixture on each plate and top with a monkfish fillet. Garnish with lemon zest and serve immediately.

PIZZA-4-TWO

From the kitchen of Peter Wallace

This is our son Peter's recipe for two different kinds of pizza he proudly prepares for his friends and family. These are obviously great for a dinner for two, but they're equally good for lunch or for a cocktail snack when you're entertaining friends. Peter says not to worry if the pizzas are not perfectly round when you press out the dough, because "it's the taste that counts." To save time, Peter often prepares several of the thin flat crusts at one time and then freezes them in large plastic bags until needed—at which point he becomes the household pizza hero.

Serves 2

- 1 ball frozen pizza dough (about 9 ounces)
- 1 teaspoon extra-virgin olive oil

PIZZA MARGHERITA

- 1 prepared crust (see above)
- ½ cup favorite tomato sauce or pizza sauce, homemade or store-bought
- ⅓ cup shredded buffalo mozzarella
- Fresh basil leaves, torn

WHITE MUSHROOM PIZZA

- 1 prepared crust (see above)
- 1 tablespoon unsalted butter
- 1 garlic clove, finely chopped
- Two 8-ounce packages sliced assorted mushrooms
- 1 tablespoon dry white wine
- 1 tablespoon finely chopped fresh flat-leaf parsley or 1 teaspoon dried
- Coarse salt and freshly ground pepper
- ¼ cup shredded fontina cheese
- Drizzle of truffle oil (optional)

1. Place the frozen pizza dough in a bowl, coat with the oil, and cover with plastic wrap. Allow to come to room temperature and rise for at least 4 hours or overnight.

2. Center the rack in the oven and preheat the oven to 450°F. Transfer the dough to a lightly floured work surface. Using your palm, gently flatten the dough and divide into two balls of equal size, each about the size of a tennis ball. Using your fingers, stretch and flatten the balls into even disks.

3. Meanwhile, heat a large cast-iron skillet over medium-high heat. One at a time, place each round in the center of the skillet and cook until the bottom is golden and partially cooked, 3 to 4 minutes. Transfer the crusts to a large, heavy baking sheet. Top the crusts with your toppings of choice and bake according to the following directions.

continued on page 150

TIP
You can also keep slices of pepperoni or prosciutto in the freezer for easy toppings.

continued from page 148

PIZZA MARGHERITA

Makes 1 pizza

Drop the sauce by spoonfuls over the prepared crust and, using the back of a large wooden spoon, gently spread it around. Scatter the mozzarella over the surface of the pizza. Bake until the crust is deep golden brown, 10 to 14 minutes. Remove the pizza from the oven and garnish with the torn fresh basil leaves.

WHITE MUSHROOM PIZZA

Makes 1 pizza

In a large skillet, heat the butter over medium-high heat until melted. Add the garlic and cook, stirring, until fragrant and softened, about 3 minutes. Add the mushrooms and cook, stirring frequently, until well browned, about 6 minutes. Stir in the wine and scrape up any browned bits of mushrooms in the pan. Continue to cook, stirring, until no liquid remains in the pan. Stir in the parsley and season to taste with salt and pepper.

Sprinkle the mushroom mixture over the prepared crust and then sprinkle the cheese evenly over the mushrooms. Bake until the cheese is melted and the crust is deep golden brown, 10 to 12 minutes. Remove from the oven and drizzle the pizza with a little truffle oil, if you like.

PRIME STEAK SANDWICH

From the kitchen of Lobel's of New York

Chris was taking me on a tour of Manhattan's Upper East Side, showing me where he grew up and went to school at P.S. 6, when we stopped in front of the historic Lobel's meat market and told me how, as a young boy, he would stand and admire the aging meat in the display locker facing Madison Avenue. We went inside, met the Lobel family, and learned more about this institution. I was thrilled when the Lobels shared this recipe with me, which happens to be the single most popular food offering at Yankee Stadium. At Lobel's, they make their own demi-glace "sauce," as they call it, and their own in-house rub. In your house, you should substitute a favorite brand of barbecue sauce and rub. And if you stop into Lobel's, tell them Chris and I sent you!

Serves 2

FOR THE STEAK

One 6-ounce strip loin steak, thinly sliced

2 tablespoons mild barbecue sauce

1 teaspoon barbecue rub

FOR THE ONION STRAWS

1 medium yellow onion, cut into thin strips (about ⅔ cup)

1 cup whole milk

1 cup all-purpose flour

½ cup cornstarch

Coarse salt and freshly ground pepper

Vegetable oil, for frying

FOR THE SANDWICHES

2 fresh brioche buns

1. **TO MAKE THE STEAK:** In a medium skillet over medium-high heat, combine the slices of steak, barbecue sauce, and rub and cook until the steak is medium rare, 2 to 3 minutes. Transfer the steak to a cutting board and cover loosely with foil to keep warm. Reserve any extra sauce left in the pan for assembling the sandwiches.

2. **TO MAKE THE ONION STRAWS:** In a large bowl, soak the onion slices in the milk for 15 minutes. Drain.

3. In a large, shallow plate, combine the flour and cornstarch and season with salt and pepper. Dredge the onions thoroughly in the mixture.

4. In a large cast-iron skillet, heat 2 inches of oil over medium-high heat until about 375°F. Shake any excess flour off the onion strips and fry them until golden and puffed, about 3 minutes. Drain on a paper towel and season to taste with salt and pepper.

5. **TO ASSEMBLE THE SANDWICHES:** On the brioche buns, pile the beef, a little additional sauce, and fried onion straws, and enjoy.

SALMON PACKETS WITH LEMON AND TARRAGON

Use this recipe as a guideline and feel free to substitute other kinds of fish or herbs, depending on what you have on hand. For instance, sometimes when I am pressed for time, I just take a handful of raw spinach and put it on the bottom of the parchment paper, place a lemon slice with a little lemon juice and oil on top, and lay the salmon fillet to finish.

Serves 2

8 to 10 asparagus spears, about 6 inches long, halved lengthwise

1 large radish, thinly sliced

Two 6-ounce skinless salmon fillets

Coarse salt and freshly ground pepper

¼ cup thinly sliced red onion (optional)

1 tablespoon finely grated lemon zest

1½ teaspoons lemon juice

1½ teaspoons finely chopped fresh tarragon or ½ teaspoon dried

2 teaspoons extra-virgin olive oil

1. Adjust the rack to the upper middle of the oven and preheat the oven to 400°F. Cut two 12- to 15-inch squares of parchment paper and spread them on a work surface.

2. Fold each in half to form a crease. Divide the asparagus and the radish between the two packets, arranging the vegetables equally over both sides of the crease.

3. Lay the salmon fillets on top of the vegetables. Season the fish with salt and pepper to taste.

4. In a small bowl, toss together the onion, if using, with the lemon zest, lemon juice, tarragon, and 1 teaspoon of the oil. Spoon the mixture evenly on top of the two salmon fillets.

5. Fold the parchment over the ingredients to enclose, making overlapping pleats to seal.

6. Transfer the packets to a baking sheet. Bake until the salmon is cooked through and the vegetables are tender, 12 to 15 minutes. Unfold the packets, drizzle with the remaining 1 teaspoon oil, and serve.

VENISON TENDERLOIN WITH BLACKBERRY GLAZE

When my friend and neighbor Angela Newnam was moving, she had a whole freezer filled with different cuts of venison. I was honored when she gave me some venison tenderloins as a farewell present. I had some blackberries on hand and thought they might make a rich, colorful sauce. Angela and I talk a lot by phone and our guest bedroom is hers whenever she comes back to D.C. Please keep sending me these tenderloins, my dear friend.

Serves 2

- 1 cup dry red wine
- ½ cup orange juice
- ¼ cup extra-virgin olive oil
- 1 scallion, white and tender green parts only, finely chopped
- 3 bay leaves
- ½ teaspoon freshly ground pepper
- One 1-pound venison tenderloin
- 1 tablespoon unsalted butter, melted
- Coarse salt
- 1½ cups fresh or thawed frozen blackberries
- ½ cup seedless blackberry jam
- ¼ cup port

1. In a large nonreactive bowl, whisk together the wine, orange juice, oil, scallions, bay leaves, and pepper to make a marinade. Place the tenderloin in a large plastic bag and pour the marinade over it. Squeeze excess air from the bag and seal it. Refrigerate the venison overnight or up to 24 hours, turning the bag occasionally to coat.

2. Remove the venison, draining off and discarding the marinade, and allow the meat to come to room temperature, about 30 minutes. Meanwhile, preheat the oven to 375°F.

3. Lightly oil a small roasting pan, one just large enough to hold the tenderloin. Brush the meat all over with the melted butter and season with salt and pepper. Scatter about one-third of the blackberries over the meat (they will mostly fall to the side). Reserve the remaining blackberries for serving.

4. Roast the venison until an instant-read thermometer inserted halfway into the center of the tenderloin reads 125°F for rare, about 20 minutes.

5. Transfer the tenderloin to a cutting board and cover loosely with foil to rest.

6. In a small saucepan, combine the roasted blackberries with the blackberry jam and the port to make a glaze. Cook over medium heat, stirring occasionally, until the jam dissolves.

7. To serve, slice the venison against the grain and arrange on a warmed platter. Drizzle the glaze over the meat, garnish with the reserved uncooked blackberries, and serve.

TIP
Venison's delicately gamy flavor comes through best when the meat is not cooked beyond medium rare.

Pork Chops with Glazed Sweet Onions

Chops are an excellent idea for a two-person meal because it's a meaty dish that's easy to do for a couple but quite challenging (not to mention costly) to do for a crowd. I say take advantage of an opportunity to make dinner for two and showcase a hearty chop as the centerpiece of supper. The sweet-and-sour caramelized onions really make this quick skillet supper. Serve the pork chops with creamy polenta and roasted Brussels sprouts, if you like.

Serves 2

Two 1-pound bone-in pork loin chops (about ¾ inch thick)

¼ cup extra-virgin olive oil

2 teaspoons finely chopped fresh thyme or 1 teaspoon dried

Coarse salt and freshly ground pepper

1 medium red onion, cut into ¼-inch rounds (about ⅔ cup)

¼ cup red wine vinegar

1½ teaspoons sugar

1. Wash the pork chops and pat them dry with paper towels. Transfer the pork chops to a large nonreactive bowl and add 2 tablespoons of the oil and 1 teaspoon of the thyme. Season with salt and pepper. Cover the bowl and marinate at room temperature for 20 minutes.

2. Place the onion slices in a medium bowl and season with a little salt and pepper. Pour in 1 tablespoon of the oil and toss to coat. In a small bowl, whisk together the vinegar, sugar, and the remaining 1 teaspoon thyme, and set aside.

3. In a large, heavy skillet, heat the remaining 1 tablespoon oil over medium-high heat. Add the chops and cook until golden, 3 to 5 minutes per side. Transfer the chops to a platter. Brush the chops on both sides with half of the vinegar mixture, loosely cover them with aluminum foil, and let rest.

4. Add the onions and the remaining vinegar mixture to the skillet and, over medium heat, cook, stirring frequently, until the onions absorb all of the liquid and become golden and glazed, 6 to 8 minutes.

5. To serve, divide the onion mixture between two plates and lay the pork chops on top.

TIP

A really nice classic side dish for these chops is homemade applesauce. Simply core, peel, and slice two apples, combine with a cinnamon stick and a lemon peel in a small pot, and cover with water. Boil for about 8 minutes or until tender, drain (discard the cinnamon stick and lemon peel), return to the pan, and coarsely mash.

VEAL CHOPS WITH WILD MUSHROOMS

After a long day meeting various deadlines, Chris and I find that these two thick veal chops are incredibly filling and satisfying. The elegant mixture of wild mushrooms and sweet cipollini onions dress up the supper. If time is limited, just serve with some sautéed potatoes alongside.

Serves 2

- 2 meaty 12-ounce veal rib chops (about 1½ inches thick)
  Coarse salt and freshly ground pepper
- 1 teaspoon dried thyme
- 10 small cipollini onions, peeled
  Pinch of sugar
- 1 tablespoon unsalted butter
- 1 tablespoon extra-virgin olive oil
- 2 large heads garlic, unpeeled and halved horizontally
- 3 cups stemmed chopped wild mushrooms (about ¾ pound)
- 3 cups stemmed quartered button mushrooms (about ¾ pound)
- 1 cup dry red wine

1. Wash the veal chops and pat them dry with paper towels. Trim the chops and set aside the fat. Season the chops on both sides with salt and pepper and the thyme.

2. Place the onions in a small saucepan and pour in enough water to fill the pan halfway. Add a pinch of salt and the sugar to the water. Heat the onions over medium-low heat until the water has nearly evaporated, shaking the pan occasionally to keep the onions from burning, about 15 minutes. Remove the onions from the heat, drain them, and set aside to cool.

3. In a large, heavy skillet over medium-high heat, combine the butter and oil. When hot, add the veal fat trimmings and garlic and cook until very fragrant, about 5 minutes. Add the veal chops to the pan. Cook for 10 minutes, then turn the chops over, baste with the pan juices, and continue cooking until the chops are tender and still slightly rare, 10 to 15 minutes more. Transfer the chops, trimmings, and garlic to a cutting board and loosely cover with foil.

4. In the same skillet over medium-high heat, cook both the mushrooms with a pinch of salt until softened and beginning to brown, about 5 minutes. Add the wine, scrape up any browned bits from the pan, and cook until the liquid is reduced by half, about 20 minutes. Taste and adjust the seasoning with salt and pepper, if needed.

5. Reduce the heat to medium-low, add the onions to the pan with the mushrooms, and gently reheat. Add the veal chops to the pan just to thoroughly rewarm the chops.

6. To serve, transfer the chops to warm plates and divide the mushrooms, onions, and pan juices evenly over both chops.

VALENTINE'S DINNER FOR TWO

If your path to your lover's heart, like mine, is through the stomach, then this simple fondue dinner for two is your answer. Skip the crowded restaurants and make your own cozy Valentine's supper at home with nothing but finger foods. Indulge all of your senses with this satisfying yet not too filling meal. I hope these suggestions get you in the lovin' mood!

CAVIAR WITH RUFFLED POTATO CHIPS

A very pleasant recent discovery in our kitchen is that caviar needn't be excessively expensive: American sturgeon caviar, a cousin of the Russian variety, is firm with a sweet, buttery-nutty flavor and less than half the price. You can find it in gourmet groceries and online. It is a perfect little splurge for a special occasion.

Serves 2

- 6 large ruffled potato chips, unbroken
- 2 tablespoons crème fraîche
- 2 tablespoons American farmed beluga caviar
- 8 fresh chives, cut into 2-inch-long pieces

Arrange the potato chips on a medium platter and spoon about 1 teaspoon crème fraîche onto each chip, then 1 teaspoon caviar on top of the cream. Gently press 2 crisscrossed chives into the top of the caviar on each chip and serve at once.

CLASSIC CHEESE FONDUE

I think fondue never goes out of style, and indeed, it's popular once again. This recipe is one to enjoy with someone you love, and I promise it will be memorable. It is especially nice because you get to use your hands. Also, this is a last-minute experience, as you make everything on the spot and then sit down to eat it. Gruyère makes the cheese sauce sweet and nutty, while sharp cheddar adds zest. Serve the fondue with cubes of good bread, sliced apples, small boiled potatoes, thick cubes of ham, and lightly steamed broccoli and cauliflower for dipping, if you like.

Serves 2

1 garlic clove, halved

8 ounces Gruyere cheese, grated

4 ounces aged sharp cheddar cheese, grated

½ cup dry white wine

2 teaspoons cornstarch

1 teaspoon lemon juice

2 teaspoons kirsch, brandy, or cognac

Coarse salt and freshly ground pepper

Rub the inside of a cheese fondue pot or medium enameled cast-iron casserole dish with the garlic clove; discard the garlic. Combine the Gruyère and cheddar with the wine, cornstarch, and lemon juice in the fondue pot and cook over medium heat, stirring occasionally, until the cheeses begin to melt, about 5 minutes. Add the kirsch and a generous pinch each of salt and pepper and continue to cook, stirring gently, until creamy and smooth, about 10 minutes; don't overcook the fondue or it will get stringy. Serve immediately.

BLACK-AND-WHITE CHOCOLATE-DIPPED STRAWBERRIES

When you combine chocolate with strawberries, you have a bona fide gourmet double threat. Although February is not strawberry season, the slightly under-ripe ones we do get in winter actually hold up well when dipped in chocolate. Always allow the strawberries to come to room temperature prior to dipping, and then place them on waxed paper to set. This part of your Valentine's dinner for two you can do ahead!

Makes 1 dozen chocolate-dipped strawberries

- 8 ounces bittersweet chocolate
- 8 ounces white chocolate
- 12 fresh strawberries, stems attached

1. Place each kind of chocolate in a separate small nonreactive bowl. Set each bowl over a saucepan of simmering water or a double boiler. Stir occasionally until the chocolate is melted, 3 to 5 minutes. Remove from the heat.

2. Line a baking sheet with waxed paper. One at a time, holding the stem, dip each strawberry in chocolate, twirling to coat, then transfer the berry to the waxed paper.

TIP
Refrigerate the chocolate-dipped strawberries for at least 15 minutes, but no more than 1 hour, to set the chocolate. (Strawberries should not be stored in the refrigerator for longer than 1 hour as condensation drops may collect on the chocolate.) Pull them out of the refrigerator and serve.

VEGETARIAN AND GLUTEN-FREE SUPPERS

I decided to create a chapter of vegetarian and gluten-free suppers because our family, just like so many of yours, has members who prefer to eat like this. And so I am faced with what to prepare on holidays or whenever our vegetarian and gluten-free family members are here for a visit, and I've put a lot of thought into making satisfying meals without the meat or without the wheat, or sometimes both.

I not only dedicate this chapter to our daughter Megan, a vegetarian, and her lovely husband Miguel, who is gluten-free, but also to everyone who is faced with menu planning for busy weeknights or special occasions. More and more when I go out with friends I hear about their wheat allergies, or how they feel better about eating more vegetarian dishes to get their proteins and daily nutrients.

I know that combining a vegetarian and gluten-free lifestyle is a big step, but I'm fairly persuaded by my friends and family and by testing these recipes myself that eating less wheat, more whole grains, and more vegetables makes you feel vibrant and healthy. To prove the point, in the Wallace household I dedicate at least two nights a week to main dishes that are hearty and fulfilling, either without the meat, without the wheat, and oftentimes without either one. It is very satisfying to get creative and make healthy suppers with so much wonderful produce and other fresh ingredients.

BLACK BEAN BURGERS WITH CHIPOTLE MAYO

Even your meat eaters will love these spicy, vegetable-loaded burgers. You can make them like a traditional hamburger, skipping the chipotle mayo and instead finishing them with lettuce, onion, melted cheese, and pickles on toasted buns. The burgers can be frozen up to 3 weeks in advance so you just have to prepare the mayo before serving.

Serves 8

FOR THE BLACK BEAN BURGERS

- 2 tablespoons extra-virgin olive oil
- 1 large red bell pepper, diced (about 1½ cups)
- 4 to 5 scallions, white and tender green parts only, thinly sliced (about ½ cup)
- ½ cup frozen corn kernels, thawed
- 4 garlic cloves, minced
- Two 15-ounce cans black beans, rinsed and drained
- 1½ teaspoons ground cumin
- ½ teaspoon crushed red pepper flakes
  Coarse salt and freshly ground pepper
- ⅔ cup plain dried bread crumbs
- 3 tablespoons chopped fresh cilantro
- 2 tablespoons sour cream or Greek yogurt
- 1 large egg, beaten

FOR THE CHIPOTLE MAYO

- ½ cup mayonnaise
- 2 teaspoons lime juice
- 1 teaspoon minced canned chipotle chili peppers in adobo sauce

FOR SERVING

Lettuce

Sliced Tomatoes

Sliced Onions

1. **TO MAKE THE BLACK BEAN BURGERS:** In a large, nonstick skillet, heat 2 teaspoons of the oil over medium-high heat. Add the bell pepper, scallions, corn, and garlic and cook, stirring, until tender and fragrant, about 5 minutes. Remove from the heat and set aside to cool slightly.

2. Add the beans to a large nonreactive bowl and use a potato masher to smash them coarsely. Add the sautéed vegetable mixture, the cumin, and red pepper flakes. Season with salt and pepper. Add ½ cup of the bread crumbs, the cilantro, sour cream, and egg, and stir until well blended.

3. Using your hands, shape the black bean mixture into eight ½-inch-thick patties. Place the patties on a waxed-paper–lined baking sheet. Cover with waxed paper and chill for at least 1 hour or until ready to cook.

4. When ready to cook, place the remaining bread crumbs in a shallow bowl. Lightly dredge each patty in the bread crumbs.

5. In a large nonstick skillet, heat 2 teaspoons of the oil over medium heat. Cook 4 patties until brown on both sides, about 5 minutes per side. Remove from the skillet; keep warm. Repeat with the remaining 2 teaspoons oil and 4 patties.

6. **TO MAKE THE CHIPOTLE MAYO:** Stir the mayonnaise, lime juice, and chipotles together in a small bowl. Cover with plastic wrap and refrigerate until ready to use.

7. Serve the black bean burgers on toasted buns with the chipotle mayo and slices of lettuce, tomato, and onion.

CORN, ROASTED PEPPER, AND LIMA CASSEROLE

The inspiration for this dish is old-fashioned corn pudding, for which there are many recipes and traditions. Don't be fooled by the idea of corn pudding as a side dish; this is a hearty casserole that can stand on its own as a centerpiece for supper. All you need is A Simple Green Salad (page 14) and some warm rolls.

Serves 8

- 8 ears fresh corn or about 3 cups thawed frozen corn kernels
- 2 slices firm white bread, torn into 1-inch pieces
- 2 tablespoons unsalted butter, cut into small cubes
- 2 teaspoons extra-virgin olive oil
- 1 medium onion, chopped into 1-inch pieces (about 1 cup)
- 2 garlic cloves, minced
- ¼ cup jarred roasted red peppers, very well drained and minced
- 1 cup shredded mild cheddar cheese
- One 10-ounce package frozen lima beans, thawed and drained
- 1 cup evaporated milk
- 2 large eggs, lightly beaten
- ½ teaspoon coarse salt
- ¼ teaspoon freshly ground pepper
- 2 to 3 drops hot sauce

1. Lightly butter a shallow 1½-quart casserole or gratin dish. Preheat the oven to 350°F.

2. Hold each ear of corn upright in a large bowl and use a sharp knife to cut the kernels from the cobs into the bowl. With the dull side of the knife, press down along the length of each cob to extract the corn's liquid, and add that to the cut corn.

3. In the bowl of a food processor, pulse the bread until crumbs are formed, 10 to 15 seconds. Add the butter and process for 10 seconds more to butter the crumbs; scrape into a small bowl and set aside.

4. In a large skillet, heat the oil over medium heat. Add the onion and garlic and cook, stirring frequently, until tender and translucent, about 3 to 4 minutes; do not brown. Stir in the roasted peppers. Remove from the heat and let cool for 5 minutes. Add the slightly cooled onion mixture to the corn. Stir in ¾ cup of the cheese, the lima beans, the buttered crumbs, evaporated milk, eggs, salt, pepper, and hot sauce. Transfer the mixture to the prepared dish. Sprinkle the remaining ¼ cup cheese evenly over the corn mixture. Bake until puffed and golden and the custard is set, 40 to 45 minutes. Remove from the oven and let rest for 5 minutes before serving.

EGGPLANT PARMESAN ROLLS TO IMPRESS

From the kitchen of Molly Stevens

When I first spied these stuffed eggplant rolls on the cover of Bon Appétit *magazine, they were practically screaming my name—I had to make them. And they were a marvel: hearty and elegant at the same time. That was in March 2010, and ever since I have been an avid follower of their creator, Ms. Molly Stevens, an award-winning food writer and cooking teacher based in Vermont. I was thrilled when she lent me this recipe to share with you. This version saves a little time from the original preparation. The rolls are placed on the baking sheet rather than packed vertically, as Molly does. Thank you so much, Molly!*

Serves 8

- 2 medium eggplant (about 2¼ pounds), trimmed, cut lengthwise into ¼-inch slices
- Coarse salt
- Extra-virgin olive oil
- 1 bunch Swiss chard (about 1 pound), center ribs removed
- 2 large eggs
- One 15-ounce container whole-milk ricotta cheese
- 1¼ cups grated Parmesan cheese
- 2 tablespoons finely chopped fresh mint
- ¾ teaspoon freshly ground pepper
- One 15-ounce can tomato sauce
- 8 ounces fresh water-packed mozzarella cheese, drained and thinly sliced

1. Layer the eggplant slices over the bottom and sides of 2 large colanders; sprinkle generously with salt. Continue layering the the eggplant in each colander, sprinkling each layer with salt, until all the eggplant slices are used. Place each colander over a large bowl; let stand at least 30 minutes and up to 1 hour. Rinse the eggplant slices to remove excess salt; dry thoroughly with paper towels.

2. Position the oven rack 5 to 6 inches from the heat source and preheat the broiler. Line 3 large rimmed baking sheets with parchment paper. Arrange the eggplant slices in a single layer on the prepared baking sheets. Brush both sides of the eggplant slices with oil. Broil 1 sheet at a time until the eggplant slices are tender and beginning to brown, watching closely and removing them as needed if cooking too quickly, about 3 to 4 minutes per side. Let the eggplant cool while you prepare the filling.

3. Preheat the oven to 350°F.

4. Bring a large pot of salted water to boil. Add the chard to the pot and boil just until wilted, about 2 minutes. Drain and rinse in cold water to stop the cooking. Squeeze the chard very dry, then chop coarsely. Squeeze the chard dry again between paper towels. Whisk the eggs and pinch of salt in a medium bowl. Stir in the chopped chard, ricotta, 1 cup of the Parmesan, the mint, and pepper.

continued on page 168

continued from page 167

5. Lightly oil a 15 × 10-inch glass baking dish. Spread half of the tomato sauce evenly over the bottom of the dish. Divide the chard-ricotta filling among the eggplant slices, placing about 1 heaping tablespoon in center of each. Starting at the short end, loosely roll up each eggplant slice to enclose the filling. Arrange the rolls, seam-side down, on top of the sauce in the dish. Spoon the remaining tomato sauce over the rolls. Arrange the mozzarella slices in a single layer on top of the rolls, then sprinkle with the remaining ¼ cup Parmesan. The dish can be assembled up to this point and refrigerated, covered, until ready to bake.

6. Bake, covered with foil, until heated through, about 30 minutes if freshly made or 40 minutes if refrigerated. Uncover and bake until brown in spots and the sauce is bubbling, 15 to 20 minutes longer. Serve hot.

FRITTATA FULLY LOADED

Who says a frittata is only for breakfast? This veggie-laden recipe is a perfect supper, especially when you add Sweet Potato Wedges (page 217) on the side.

Serves 8

- 2 cups loosely packed baby spinach
- 2 teaspoons unsalted butter
- 8 ounces button mushrooms, thinly sliced
- 1 medium red bell pepper, thinly sliced (about 1 cup)
- 1 medium green bell pepper, thinly sliced (about 1 cup)
- 1 medium shallot, thinly sliced (about ¼ cup)
- 1 teaspoon finely chopped fresh thyme or ⅓ teaspoon dried

  Coarse salt and freshly ground pepper
- 8 eggs, beaten
- ¼ cup whole milk
- ¼ cup grated Parmesan cheese
- ¼ cup shredded cheddar cheese

1. In a 10-inch ovenproof skillet, bring ½ cup of water to a boil over moderately high heat. Add the spinach and cook, stirring, until wilted, about 1 minute. Using tongs, transfer the spinach to a colander. Gently squeeze the greens dry and coarsely chop them. Wipe out the skillet.

2. Position the oven rack in the top third of the oven and preheat the oven to 400°F.

3. In the same skillet, heat the butter over medium heat until melted. Add the mushrooms, bell peppers, and shallot and cook, stirring, until the vegetables are tender and the liquid has evaporated, about 6 to 8 minutes. Add the chopped spinach and the thyme and cook, stirring, until hot. Season to taste with salt and pepper.

4. In a medium bowl, briskly whisk the eggs, milk, and cheeses and lightly season with salt and pepper.

5. Pour the egg mixture into the skillet with the vegetables; tilt the skillet to evenly distribute the eggs and cook over medium-low heat until set around the edges, about 3 minutes. Transfer the frittata to the oven and bake until thoroughly set, about 8 to 10 minutes. Invert the frittata onto a plate and let cool slightly. Cut into 8 wedges and serve.

Moussaka, Vegetarian-Style

This recipe is a meatless version of the classic Greek dish—bulgur is substituted for the meat and surrounded by eggplant and a spicy tomato and béchamel sauce.

Serves 8

- 6 medium Italian eggplants (about 5 pounds), peeled and cut into ½-inch slices
- ¼ cup extra-virgin olive oil
- Nonstick cooking spray
- 3 medium onions, finely chopped (about 4 cups)
- 4 garlic cloves, minced
- 1 cup bulgur
- ½ teaspoon ground allspice
- ½ teaspoon ground cinnamon
- ¼ teaspoon ground cloves
- 1 quart (4 cups) vegetable broth, homemade or store-bought
- Two 14.5-ounce cans diced tomatoes, with their juices
- 1 tablespoon finely chopped fresh oregano or 1 teaspoon dried
- 2 tablespoons unsalted butter
- ¼ cup all-purpose flour, rice flour, or almond flour
- 2 cups whole milk
- ¼ cup grated fresh Parmesan cheese
- ½ teaspoon coarse salt
- 2 large eggs, lightly beaten

1. Preheat the broiler.

2. Brush the eggplant slices with half of the oil. Place half of the eggplant slices on a foil-lined baking sheet coated with nonstick cooking spray. Broil the eggplant until browned on both sides, about 5 minutes per side. Repeat with the remaining eggplant. Set the eggplant slices aside.

3. Heat a large skillet over medium-high heat. Add the remaining oil, swirling to coat the pan. Add the onions and cook, stirring, until softened and light brown, 5 to 8 minutes. Add the garlic and cook, stirring, until fragrant and soft, about 1 minute longer. Add the bulgur and cook until lightly toasted, stirring frequently, about 3 minutes. Add the allspice, cinnamon, and cloves, and cook for 1 minute longer, stirring constantly. Stir in the broth, tomatoes with their juices, and oregano. Bring to a boil; reduce the heat to medium-low, and simmer, stirring occasionally, until thickened, about 20 minutes.

4. Melt the butter in a medium saucepan over medium heat. Add the flour; cook, whisking constantly, until well blended, about 1 minute. Gradually add the milk, stirring constantly with a whisk. Bring to a boil; reduce the heat to medium-low, and simmer, stirring frequently, until thickened, about 5 minutes more. Stir in the cheese and salt. Remove from the heat and let cool slightly, about 5 minutes. Blend the eggs into the milk mixture, stirring well with a whisk.

5. Preheat the oven to 350°F.

6. Arrange half of the eggplant in a shallow 11 × 7-inch baking dish coated with nonstick cooking spray. Spread the bulgur mixture evenly over the eggplant; arrange the remaining eggplant over the bulgur. Top with the milk mixture. Bake for 40 minutes or until beginning to bubble, then remove from the oven. Increase the temperature to 475°F. Return the dish to the oven until the top is browned, about 4 minutes. Let stand for 10 minutes before serving.

Orecchiette with Roasted Red Peppers and Spinach

The roasted red peppers and colorful cherry tomatoes collapse into a pretty, rustic sauce that is the best part of this simple supper. Serve the pasta with good crusty Italian bread to soak up all of the sauce!

Serves 8

- 4 medium red bell peppers
- 1 pound orecchiette
- 6 tablespoons extra-virgin olive oil
- 1 large garlic clove, minced
- 4 cups yellow and orange cherry tomatoes, halved
- 6 tablespoons apple cider vinegar
- 3 tablespoons sugar
- ½ teaspoon freshly ground pepper
- ¼ teaspoon dried marjoram
- ¼ teaspoon dried rosemary
- ¼ teaspoon dried thyme
- 3 cups loosely packed baby spinach, tough stems removed
- 3 cups loosely packed basil leaves
- 1½ cups grated Parmesan cheese (optional), for serving

1. Adjust the oven rack to the upper portion of the oven. Preheat the broiler.

2. Halve the bell peppers lengthwise, discarding seeds and membranes. Place the pepper halves, skin-side up, on a foil-lined baking sheet. Gently flatten them with the palm of your hand. Broil for 15 minutes, or until the peppers are slightly charred. Transfer the charred peppers to a plastic bag, seal it, and let stand for 10 minutes. Then peel the peppers and chop them into ½-inch strips. Set aside.

3. Cook the pasta until al dente according to package directions. Drain.

4. Heat 1 teaspoon of the oil in a large nonstick skillet over medium-high heat. Add 1 teaspoon of the garlic and cook until just fragrant, about 30 seconds. Add the tomatoes and cook until they are tender, stirring occasionally, about 4 minutes. Add the chopped bell peppers and cook for about 1 minute. Remove from the heat and set aside.

5. In a small bowl, whisk the remaining garlic with the vinegar, the remaining oil, the sugar, pepper, marjoram, rosemary, and thyme and set aside.

6. Add the pasta and the vinegar mixture to the red pepper mixture in the pan. Using tongs, toss well to coat. Stir in the spinach and basil for a minute or two to just wilt, then serve the pasta immediately, topped with plenty of grated cheese, if you like.

PASTA PRIMAVERA

From the kitchen of Pauline Dora Bourgeois

This recipe is Chris's sister Pauline's version of the quintessential colorful summer pasta dish, and it includes lots and lots of fresh vegetables and herbs. Pauline says she likes to purchase interesting kinds of pastas to make it fun and new. Any thick-style noodle works well to hold the sauce and crisp vegetables—I like mafaldine, an artisanally crafted thick noodle with ridged edges. Pauline also says this is the way she uses up all the assorted vegetables left over from other meals. The recipe needs a total of 7 cups of different colorful vegetables, so you get to choose your favorites. The easiest way to make this: Start your pasta water while you're finishing the vegetables, so that you can transfer the noodles with tongs directly from their boiling water and into the hot skillet with the veggies. Easy!

Serves 8

- 24 ounces mafaldine or other short interestingly shaped pasta of choice
- ¼ cup extra-virgin olive oil
- 1 small onion, thinly sliced (about ⅔ cup)
- 3 garlic cloves, chopped
  Coarse salt and freshly ground pepper
- 5 medium plum tomatoes, diced (about 2 cups)
- 8 ounces small button mushrooms, thinly sliced
- 1 cup thin green beans, trimmed and thinly sliced
- 6 asparagus spears, tips and stalks only, thinly sliced (about 1 cup)
- 5 to 7 medium carrots, peeled and thinly sliced (about 1 cup)
- 3 medium zucchini, sliced into 1-inch matchsticks (about 2 cups)
- 1 cup fresh or thawed frozen snow peas
- 1 cup frozen peas, thawed
- 1 tablespoon unsalted butter
  Crushed red pepper flakes
- 1 cup coarsely chopped mixed fresh herbs, baby spinach, or arugula, or a combination based on what you have on hand
- ½ cup toasted pine nuts
- 1 cup grated Parmesan cheese

1. In a large pot of boiling salted water, cook the pasta until just al dente, 7 to 8 minutes. Meanwhile, start cooking the vegetables at the same time.

2. In a large skillet, heat the oil over medium-low heat. Add the onion and garlic and cook, stirring, until soft and fragrant, about 5 minutes. Season well with salt and pepper. Add the tomatoes, mushrooms, green beans, asparagus, carrots, zucchini, and snow peas and cook until just tender, taking care not to overcook, about 4 minutes. Add the peas, butter, and red pepper flakes to taste and cook for 2 minutes longer, stirring to combine well.

3. Using large tongs, lift the cooked pasta out of the water and add it to the cooked vegetables along with a little of the pasta water. Toss to combine all the ingredients. Toss in the pine nuts and stir to mix well. Remove the primavera from the heat.

4. Using the same tongs, transfer some of the pasta to warmed large pasta bowls and top with the vegetables and their juices. Sprinkle with the herbs and cheese. Serve immediately with good, crusty bread, if you like.

PORTOBELLO CAP LASAGNAS

When I prepare this quick gluten-free and vegetarian dish, I sometimes replace the spinach with chopped kale or Swiss chard—whatever leafy green you have on hand will work just fine. Not only is the casserole a beauty, but it is so addictive that in our house it's always gone the next day. It is good cold for lunch, too.

Serves 8

16	medium portobello mushroom caps (about three 6-ounce packs)
2½	tablespoons extra-virgin olive oil
	Coarse salt and freshly ground pepper
3	medium shallots, finely chopped (about ¼ cup)
2	medium garlic cloves, minced
One	10-ounce bag frozen chopped spinach, thawed and well drained
One	15-ounce container whole-milk ricotta cheese
1	large egg, beaten
½	teaspoon ground nutmeg
3	cups store-bought marinara sauce
2	cups shredded mozzarella cheese
¼	cup finely grated Pecorino Romano cheese
½	cup coarsely chopped fresh basil or flat-leaf parsley, for garnish

1. Position the rack in the upper portion of the oven. Preheat the oven to 425°F.

2. Brush the mushroom caps with 1 tablespoon of the oil and lightly season with salt and pepper. Place them on a baking sheet, stem-side down, and roast until they have released their juices, 10 to 12 minutes. Remove from the oven and place on paper towels, stem-side down, to drain and cool.

3. In a medium skillet over medium-high heat, warm the remaining 1½ tablespoons oil. Add the shallots and cook until caramelized, about 5 minutes. Add the garlic and continue to cook until softened, about 1 minute longer. Add the spinach, stirring to combine the vegetables well.

4. In a medium bowl, combine the ricotta, egg, spinach mixture, nutmeg, a pinch of salt, and a few turns of pepper, stirring to mix well.

5. Reduce the oven temperature to 375°F and leave the rack in the upper portion of the oven. Spread half of the marinara sauce on the bottom of an ovenproof baking dish. Lay the mushrooms on top in a single layer. Using a tablespoon, heap some of the cheese filling on top of each mushroom. Top with the mozzarella and Pecorino cheeses and bake, uncovered, until the casserole is bubbling and golden on top, 35 to 40 minutes. Let cool slightly, then garnish with the basil. Warm the remaining sauce and serve at the table.

6. To serve, place a little of the sauce on a plate, then top with a mushroom or two.

TIP
You can make this casserole 1 day ahead of serving. Just refrigerate, tightly covered with aluminum foil, until it's ready to bake.

SPAGHETTI SIMPLE SUMMER-STYLE WITH BROILED FRESH TOMATOES

When large beefsteak tomatoes are abundant at the end of summer, this is a dish I cannot wait to make. It is so elemental to prepare and satisfying—pasta with a fresh tomato sauce baked with cheese. Toss a large green salad and make some loaded garlic bread to finish this simple supper.

Serves 8

- 24 ounces spaghetti (one and a half 16-ounce packages)

  Nonstick cooking spray

- 6 large beefsteak tomatoes (about 1½ pounds), cut into 4 thick slices each

  Coarse salt and freshly ground pepper

- 1 pound fresh mozzarella cheese, grated
- ½ cup grated Parmesan cheese, plus more, shaved, for serving
- ½ cup extra-virgin olive oil
- 4 garlic cloves, finely chopped
- ½ teaspoon crushed red pepper flakes
- 1½ cups fresh basil leaves, torn, plus more for serving

1. Preheat the broiler.

2. In a large, heavy stockpot, cook the pasta to al dente according to package directions. Drain the pasta and return it to the pot.

3. Meanwhile, coat a large rimmed baking sheet with nonstick cooking spray and arrange the tomato slices in a single layer; season with salt and pepper to taste. Divide the mozzarella evenly among the slices, scattering it over the top of each. Divide the Parmesan evenly among the slices, scattering it on top of the mozzarella on each. Broil until the cheese is bubbly and golden, 3 to 5 minutes.

4. In a medium saucepan, warm the oil with the garlic and crushed red pepper over medium heat until fragrant, 1 to 2 minutes. Remove from the heat.

5. Add the garlic oil and torn basil to the pasta and toss together using tongs to coat. Season to taste with salt and pepper. Serve the pasta topped with a tomato and cheese stack, plus additional basil and shaved Parmesan.

SOUTHWEST QUINOA SALAD

Here is a recipe that uses the super-grain quinoa, combining it with vegetables and beans to make a complete dish. Slice some avocados and limes, then warm corn tortillas and prepare a kind of "taco bar" at the table, so each person can garnish his or her own quinoa salad to taste.

Serves 8

- 2¼ cups water
- 1½ cups quinoa, rinsed and drained
- ½ teaspoon coarse salt, plus more for the dressing
- 1 cup frozen shelled edamame, thawed and drained
- 1 cup canned corn, drained
- 1 cup canned black beans, rinsed and drained
- 1 medium red bell pepper, chopped (about ⅔ cup)
- 6 tablespoons lime juice, plus more to taste
- 6 tablespoons extra-virgin olive oil
- 1 garlic clove, minced
- ½ teaspoon chili powder
- ½ teaspoon ground cumin
   Freshly ground pepper
- 1 cup finely chopped fresh cilantro

1. To a medium saucepan, add the water, quinoa, and salt. Bring to a boil over medium-high heat; reduce the heat to low, cover, and cook until the water is absorbed and the quinoa is light and fluffy, 15 to 20 minutes. Remove from the heat and let rest, covered, for 10 minutes. Use a fork to fluff the quinoa, then pour into a large bowl and let cool to room temperature.

2. Add the edamame, corn, black beans, and bell pepper to the quinoa. Gently toss to combine. Cover with plastic wrap and set aside.

3. To make the dressing, in a medium bowl, whisk the lime juice, oil, garlic, chili powder, and cumin, and season with salt and pepper.

4. Pour the dressing over the quinoa mixture and toss gently to combine. Right before serving, add the cilantro and mix again. Taste and adjust the seasonings with more salt, pepper, or lime juice, if desired. This dish can be refrigerated up to 5 days, tightly covered with plastic wrap. Let come to room temperature before serving.

SPINACH SOUFFLÉ

From the kitchen of Megan Wallace

Julia Child is the inspiration for our daughter Megan's spinach soufflé recommendation, but we adapted Child's classic version. To make hers gluten-free, Megan substitutes cornstarch for flour. It is classic and elegant, but the best part is that it's easy. Feel free to use any hard cheese you like or have handy in place of the sharp cheddar. Serve with a salad of shredded raw veggies (page 15), if you like.

Serves 8

- 2 tablespoons unsalted butter, at room temperature, plus more for baking dish
- ⅓ cup grated Parmesan cheese
- 5 cups packed spinach (about 5 ounces), trimmed and washed
- 2 tablespoons all-purpose flour
- ¾ cup plus 2 tablespoons whole milk
- ½ cup grated sharp cheddar cheese
- Coarse salt and freshly ground pepper
- 2 large eggs, separated, plus 2 large egg whites

1. Preheat the oven to 375°F.

2. Butter a round deep 1-quart baking dish and dust with the Parmesan; set aside. In a large skillet, heat 2 tablespoons water over medium-high heat. Add the spinach and cook, stirring constantly, until wilted, about 4 minutes. Transfer to a strainer to cool; press to release excess liquid.

3. In a medium saucepan, melt the butter over medium heat until bubbling. Add the flour and whisk until a paste forms. Continue to cook, whisking constantly, until pale blond in color, 2 to 3 minutes. Gradually whisk in the milk. Cook, whisking, until any lumps are gone and the mixture is thickened, 3 to 5 minutes. Remove from the heat. Stir in the cheddar cheese until melted; season with salt and pepper. Transfer the mixture to a large bowl.

4. In a food processor, pulse the cooked spinach and egg yolks until well combined. Add ¼ cup of the milk mixture; pulse until blended. Stir the spinach mixture into the remaining milk mixture in the bowl. (You can prepare the soufflé up to 4 hours ahead up to this point. To store, press plastic wrap directly against the surface of the mixture and keep at room temperature.)

5. In a large bowl, using an electric mixer, beat the egg whites and a pinch of salt on medium-high speed until stiff peaks form (do not overbeat), about 3 minutes. In 2 additions, gently fold the egg whites into the spinach mixture. Pour the batter into the prepared dish and bake until the soufflé is tall, browned, and firm to the touch, about 35 minutes. (Do not open the oven during first 25 minutes of baking or your soufflé will fall.) Serve immediately, piping hot.

SUMMER SQUASH AND ZUCCHINI CASSEROLE

Cilantro and Greek yogurt add a special zest to this classic dish. You can prepare this casserole and refrigerate it, covered tightly with plastic wrap, for one day in advance—just be sure to let it come to room temperature prior to baking. Serve with A Simple Green Salad (page 14), if you like.

Serves 8

- 1 pound yellow squash, cleaned, trimmed, and cut into ½-inch cubes (about 2 cups)
- 1 pound zucchini, cleaned, trimmed, and cut into ½-inch cubes (about 2 cups)
- Nonstick cooking spray
- Coarse salt and freshly ground pepper
- 1 cup grated sharp cheddar cheese
- ½ cup plain Greek yogurt or sour cream
- 4 scallions, white and tender green parts only, coarsely chopped (about ⅓ cup)
- ¼ cup mayonnaise
- 2 tablespoons finely chopped fresh cilantro
- 1½ cups panko bread crumbs
- 1½ tablespoons unsalted butter, cut into small cubes
- ½ teaspoon Hungarian paprika

1. Preheat the oven to 425°F.

2. Line a large baking sheet with parchment paper and spread the squash and zucchini cubes out on it. Spray the vegetables with nonstick cooking spray and season generously with salt and pepper. Roast the vegetables until they are just tender and beginning to brown, about 15 minutes. Let them rest until cool enough to handle, about 10 minutes. Reduce the oven temperature to 350°F.

3. In a large bowl, combine the roasted vegetables with the cheese, sour cream, scallions, mayonnaise, and cilantro; mix well and season to taste with salt and pepper.

4. Lightly spray a shallow 2½- to 3-quart casserole dish with nonstick cooking spray, then spread the squash mixture into the dish. Scatter the panko and the butter cubes evenly over the top and then sprinkle with the paprika. Cover tightly with foil and bake the casserole until set, 15 to 20 minutes. Uncover and bake until the filling is bubbling and the top is golden, about 15 minutes more. Let the casserole cool for 5 minutes before serving.

Tofu and Veggie Stir-Fry with Soba Noodles

Tofu adds mellow, mild protein to the colorful vegetables in this easy weeknight stir-fry. You can find gluten-free versions of soba noodles and soy sauce in most groceries, if you prefer those.

Serves 8

- 2 pounds silken tofu
- ⅔ cup water
- ⅔ cup oyster sauce
- 1 tablespoon all-purpose flour
- 1 pound green beans, trimmed and cut in half crosswise (about 3 cups)
- 6 medium carrots, peeled and cut into ¼-inch-wide strips (about 2 cups)
- 2 tablespoons vegetable oil
- 1 medium white onion, thinly sliced (about ⅔ cup)
- 1 small red bell pepper, thinly sliced (about ⅔ cup)
- 2 garlic cloves, minced
- One 15-ounce can baby corn, drained and halved crosswise
- Freshly ground pepper
- One 8.8-ounce package soba noodles
- 2 to 3 scallions, white and tender green parts only, cut on the diagonal into 2-inch strips, for garnish
- 1 cup soy sauce, for serving

1. Drain the tofu and pat dry with paper towels, then place in a large nonreactive bowl. Combine ⅓ cup of the water, ⅓ cup of the oyster sauce, and the flour in a small bowl and whisk to mix well. Pour over the tofu in the bowl and let marinate in the refrigerator for at least 1 hour.

2. Bring a large pot of water to boil over high heat. Add the green beans and blanch until bright green, about 2 minutes. Remove from the heat, transfer to a colander, and rinse under cold running water to stop the cooking. Repeat the procedure to blanch the carrots. Set aside.

3. Heat the oil over medium-high heat in a wok or skillet large enough to hold all of the ingredients. Add the onion and bell pepper and stir-fry for 3 minutes. Add the garlic and stir-fry for 1 minute more.

4. Using a large wooden spoon, fold in the tofu with the remaining ⅓ cup oyster sauce and the remaining ⅓ cup water, stirring gently to coat all the ingredients with the sauce, and cook to warm through, about 5 minutes. Stir in the blanched green beans and carrots and the baby corn and cook until the vegetables are heated through, about 1 minute. Season to taste with pepper.

5. Meanwhile, cook the soba noodles according to the package directions. Divide the noodles equally among eight serving plates and top with the stir-fry. Garnish with the scallions and serve with the soy sauce in a small bowl on the table.

TIP
Oyster sauce isn't traditionally vegetarian, but you can source vegetarian versions made from mushrooms in groceries and health food stores, or substitute dark soy sauce instead.

KALE AND CHARD GRATIN

In addition to making a hearty vegetarian supper, this bright green gratin is a lovely side dish for winter entertaining. I like to serve it right along with the big roasts during Christmas and watch my family dig in. It is high in fiber and packed with all the vitamins and minerals that are especially good for you. For a busy winter night, serve it alongside tomato soup, roasted tomatoes, or a lovely shredded raw vegetable salad (page 15).

Serves 8

- 1 tablespoon unsalted butter, plus more for baking dish
- Two 16-ounce bags frozen chopped kale, thawed and drained
- Coarse salt
- Two 16-ounce bags frozen Swiss chard, thawed and drained
- ¼ cup extra-virgin olive oil
- 3 cups panko bread crumbs
- ½ cup finely grated Parmesan
- 2 teaspoons fresh thyme leaves, plus 7 sprigs fresh thyme
- 2 medium shallots, sliced into ¼-inch thick rounds (about 1 cup)
- 1 cup heavy cream
- 1 cup whole milk
- 7 garlic cloves, smashed
- ⅛ teaspoon freshly ground nutmeg
- Freshly ground pepper
- 1 cup coarsely grated Gruyère cheese

1. Prepare an ice-water bath in a large bowl. Lightly butter an ovenproof 3-quart baking dish. Working in batches, blanch the kale in a pot of boiling lightly salted water until just softened, about 3 minutes. Using a slotted spoon, transfer the kale to the ice-water bath; let cool, then drain. Squeeze out as much excess water as possible by hand and transfer the kale to a work surface.

2. Repeat with the chard, blanching for 2 minutes per batch. Coarsely chop all the greens and combine in a large bowl (you should have 6 cups tightly packed greens). Separate any clumps and loosen the chopped leaves by hand.

3. Heat the oil in a medium skillet over medium heat. Add the panko and cook, stirring frequently, until golden and crispy, 8 to 10 minutes. Transfer to a large bowl; stir in the Parmesan and 1 teaspoon of the thyme leaves.

4. In a medium saucepan, melt the butter over medium-high heat. Add the shallots and cook, stirring often, until slightly softened and light golden, about 5 minutes. Transfer the shallots to the bowl with the greens. To the saucepan, add the cream, milk, garlic, and thyme sprigs; bring to a simmer. Cook until the mixture is thickened and reduced to 1½ cups, 10 to 12 minutes. Discard the thyme sprigs and garlic and stir in the nutmeg. Season the mixture with salt and pepper.

5. Preheat the oven to 400°F.

6. Pour the cream mixture over the greens and toss to evenly coat; season to taste with salt and pepper. Transfer the greens mixture to the prepared baking dish. Sprinkle the Gruyère over the greens and then top with the bread crumb mixture.

7. Cover the baking dish with foil and bake until the filling is hot, about 25 minutes. Uncover and bake until the cheese is melted, edges are bubbling, and bread crumbs are golden brown, 10 to 20 minutes longer. Garnish with the remaining 1 teaspoon thyme leaves and serve.

KALE AND SPINACH TART

We call this Remick's "smart tart" because it's filled with super-healthy super foods and he eats bags of greens daily. It's an ideal vegetarian main course in part because the crust is not only easy to make but also may be made in advance and refrigerated for a couple of days before you fill it. Just toss a large salad and everything you need for a complete meal is done! It is also gluten-free, and a crowd pleaser.

Serves 8

FOR THE FILLING

- 1 tablespoon extra-virgin olive oil
- 2 medium leeks, white and tender green parts only, sliced in half, finely chopped (about 4 cups)
- 2 garlic cloves, minced
- ¼ teaspoon crushed red pepper flakes
- One 16-ounce bag frozen chopped spinach, thawed and drained
- One 16-ounce bag frozen chopped kale, thawed and drained
- ½ cup crumbled feta cheese
- 2 large eggs, lightly beaten
- Coarse salt

FOR THE CRUST

- Nonstick cooking spray
- ¾ cup brown rice flour
- ¾ cup white rice flour
- ½ teaspoon coarse salt
- ½ teaspoon sesame seeds, lightly toasted
- ½ cup extra-virgin olive oil
- ½ cup water

1. **TO MAKE THE FILLING:** In a large pan, heat the oil over medium-high heat. Add the leeks and cook until tender and golden, about 5 minutes. Add the garlic and red pepper flakes and cook until fragrant and well combined, another 2 to 3 minutes. Transfer to a large bowl. Using your hands, squeeze any remaining water from the spinach and kale, then combine them in the bowl with the leek mixture. Set aside to cool while you make the crust.

2. Position a rack in the center of the oven and preheat the oven to 425°F. Spray a 9-inch tart pan with a removable bottom with non-stick cooking spray.

3. **TO MAKE THE CRUST:** In a medium bowl, whisk together both flours, the salt, and the sesame seeds to combine. Stir in the oil and water, then gently knead into a ball, taking care not to overhandle the dough. Place the ball of dough in the center of the prepared pan. Using your hands, press the crust out evenly, covering the bottom of the pan and about halfway up the sides.

4. Add the feta, eggs, and a dash of salt to the vegetable mixture and stir to combine. Using a large slotted spoon, transfer the filling into the crust. Bake until the tart is just set, 25 to 30 minutes. Transfer the tart to a rack to cool slightly, about 5 minutes, then unmold and transfer to a platter, cut into wedges, and serve warm or at room temperature.

SUNDAY SUPPERS

A Sunday supper used to be a frequent occasion for American families, even the ones that never attended church. These were not just any meal, but once-a-week happenings in which the whole family, including aunts, uncles, and cousins, got together to catch up and, of course, to eat.

To me, Sunday supper is still a wonderful idea because it offers a chance for families to celebrate together, ask each other for advice, and share life's lessons. Despite the fast-paced world we live in, we still need to take breaks to enjoy each other, and to model family togetherness for our kids. Sunday suppers are the best way to do it.

If you are fortunate enough to have your extended family nearby, why not resurrect this overlooked tradition? To start, try preparing a few classic family-favorite recipes, and then print them up or e-mail them to one another as keepsakes. Let the children help make menu or theme-night suggestions—like a Mexican fiesta, a pasta night, or a classic roast turkey (without having to wait for Thanksgiving).

If your family is not nearby, then start a tradition with your close friends by hosting a good old-fashioned potluck. Ask your friends and their children over so you all can create memories over your meals. Most of the recipes I share with you here in this chapter are ones that my own family treasures. Use them as a guideline to start your own "Sunday supper" tradition, seasoned with lots of love!

Fish Stew
Supper Menu

Olive Oil Grilled Bread

Italian Chopped Salad

Fish Stew

Key Lime Pie Bars

OLIVE OIL GRILLED BREAD

You can peel a whole clove of raw garlick and rub it onto the bread slices.

Serves 8

- 8 thick slices bread from a large country loaf, each about ¾ inch thick
- 8 tablespoons extra-virgin olive oil
  Coarse salt

1. Preheat the broiler.

2. Brush both sides of each piece of bread with the oil, about 1 tablespoon per slice. Sprinkle both sides with a little salt. Broil the bread, turning once, until crisp and golden on the surface but still soft inside, about 4 minutes total. Serve the toasts with the fish stew.

ITALIAN CHOPPED SALAD

Add white beans and garlic to a simple chopped salad and you've got an ideal side dish for any Italian meal. I like to serve this by prepping all of the ingredients ahead of time and then tossing them in a large bowl at the table.

Serves 8

- ¼ cup red wine vinegar
- 1 teaspoon coarse salt, plus more to taste
- 1 teaspoon freshly ground pepper, plus more to taste
- 1 cup extra-virgin olive oil
- 8 cups finely chopped romaine lettuce (about 2 medium heads)
- 8 cups finely chopped radicchio (about 2 medium heads)
- 2 cups cooked or drained, rinsed canned cannellini beans
- 2 cups small mozzarella balls, halved
- 1½ cups drained oil-packed sun-dried tomato halves, coarsely chopped
- ½ cup loosely packed fresh basil leaves, torn, for garnish

In a large wooden or other salad bowl, whisk together the vinegar, salt, and pepper. Gradually whisk in the oil to combine well. Add the lettuce, radicchio, beans, mozzarella balls, and sun-dried tomatoes. Using tongs, toss to coat. Season the salad to taste with more salt and pepper if you like. Garnish with the basil.

FISH STEW

Every Christmas Eve my children take over my kitchen and excitedly prepare an Italian-style "Feast of the Seven Fishes" for the family. I am more than thrilled to have the night before Christmas off, and always curious to see what new and interesting ways they'll come up with to prepare the seven fish dishes. This fish stew they created is often the centerpiece. If you like, you can add more shellfish to the savory broth, and devise other appetizers and recipes around this stew like our family does.

Serves 8

- 16 medium plum tomatoes or one 28-ounce can whole plum tomatoes, drained
- 1 cup extra-virgin olive oil
- 6 large garlic cloves, minced
- 1 quart (4 cups) water
- 3 cups dry white wine
- 1 tablespoon capers, rinsed
- Crushed red pepper flakes
- 1 cup cherry tomatoes, halved
- ½ cup pitted kalamata olives
- 1½ pounds clams or mussels, thoroughly scrubbed and rinsed well
- Eight 6-ounce skin-on red snapper or striped bass fillets
- Coarse salt and freshly ground pepper
- ¾ cup all-purpose flour
- 1½ pounds large shrimp (16 to 20 count), peeled and deveined, tails left on
- 3 tablespoons finely chopped fresh flat-leaf parsley or basil, or a combination

1. Preheat the oven to 300°F. Line a large baking sheet with parchment paper. Wash and quarter the plum tomatoes and arrange them, cut-side up, on the prepared baking sheet. Roast until the tomatoes are leathery but soft, 2 to 2½ hours.

2. In a large, heavy Dutch oven, heat ½ cup of the oil over medium heat. Add the garlic and cook, stirring, until golden, 2 to 3 minutes. Add the water, wine, capers, and red pepper flakes to taste. Bring the mixture to a boil, then reduce the heat to a simmer and allow the liquid to reduce to about 6 cups, about 20 minutes. Add the roasted tomatoes and cherry tomatoes along with the olives. Add the clams or mussels, cover the pot, and cook until the bivalves pop open, 5 to 8 minutes. Discard any clams that do not open. Simmer to let the flavors combine, about 5 minutes.

3. Meanwhile, season the fish on both sides with salt and pepper. Pour the flour onto a large plate and dredge the fish in the flour, shaking off any excess. Heat the remaining ½ cup oil in a large skillet over medium-high heat until nearly smoking. Fry the fish, skin-side down, until golden, 2 to 3 minutes, then flip and fry on the other side, 2 to 3 minutes more.

4. Quickly transfer the fish to the stew. Add the shrimp and continue simmering until the shrimp is bright pink and cooked through, about 3 minutes more.

5. To serve, use a slotted spoon to transfer the fish fillets into warmed wide-rimmed bowls. Top with the shellfish and the cooking liquid, then garnish with the parsley. Serve immediately.

KEY LIME PIE BARS

This recipe is both a twist on classic lemon bars and also a handy way to enjoy the flavors of Key lime pie without having to make an actual pie.

Serves 8

FOR THE CRUST

Nonstick cooking spray

16 tablespoons (2 sticks) unsalted butter, softened

½ cup confectioner's sugar, plus more for garnish

2½ cups all-purpose flour

Pinch of coarse salt

FOR THE TOPPING

4 large eggs, lightly beaten

2 cups sugar

3 tablespoons all-purpose flour

1 tablespoon finely grated lime zest

½ cup fresh key lime juice (from about 17 key limes) or ½ cup bottled key lime juice

1. **TO MAKE THE CRUST:** Preheat the oven to 350°F. Spray the bottom and sides of a 13 × 9-inch baking dish with nonstick spray.

2. In the bowl of an electric mixer, combine the butter and confectioner's sugar. Using the paddle attachment, beat on medium-high speed until light and fluffy and well combined, 2 to 3 minutes. Add the flour and salt, and beat until well combined, about another minute.

3. Using a rubber spatula, transfer the mixture to the prepared pan, spreading it out over the bottom to an even thickness. Bake until lightly golden and set, 20 to 25 minutes. Remove from the oven, and cool in the pan on a baking rack.

4. **TO MAKE THE TOPPING:** In a large mixing bowl, whisk the eggs and sugar to combine. Add the flour, whisk until just combined (the batter will be slightly lumpy), then whisk in the lime zest and lime juice until smooth. Pour the lime topping over the cooled crust, then bake until the filling is just set, rotating the dish halfway through the cooking time, about 25 minutes.

5. Transfer to a wire rack to cool completely. Use a sharp knife to cut 2 × 2-inch bars. Refrigerate the bars at least four hours or overnight before serving.

6. Serve the bars at room temperature, or slightly cool, depending on your preference—they're good both ways—garnished with confectioner's sugar just before serving.

The cookie crust dough can be prepared up to 2 days in advance, then wrapped in plastic and stored in the refrigerator. When you're ready to bake the bars, simply bring the dough to room temperature, pat into the pan, and bake. For the neatest presentation, make these bite-size: Use a sharp knife to cut 1½-inch square bites, then use a metal spatula or scraper to remove the bars from the pan and transfer to a platter. Leftover bars will keep for 2 to 3 days at room temperature, or for up to a week in the refrigerator.

Glazed Ham Supper Menu

Macaroni and Cheese

Deviled Eggs with a Twist

Glazed Ham

Sweet-and-Sour Carrots

Lemon Cupcakes

MACARONI AND CHEESE

This creamy mac 'n' cheese is unique because you do not boil the elbows before assembling it. Just put your blender to work to create the sauce, combine it with the uncooked elbows, and bake. Note that the dish is best served piping hot, right out of the oven. If you have leftovers, you'll need to mix in a tablespoon or two of water or milk per cup before reheating.

Serves 8

- 4 cups whole milk
- 2 cups ricotta cheese
- 1 teaspoon dry mustard
- 2 teaspoons coarse salt
- 1 teaspoon freshly ground pepper
- Pinch or two of cayenne pepper
- Pinch or two of freshly grated nutmeg
- 2 pounds sharp cheddar cheese, grated
- 1 pound elbow macaroni

1. Preheat the oven to 375°F. Grease a 13 × 9-inch baking dish.

2. In a blender, puree the milk, ricotta cheese, mustard, salt, pepper, cayenne, and nutmeg. In a large bowl, combine the cheddar cheese, milk mixture, and uncooked pasta. Pour into the prepared pan, cover tightly with aluminum foil, and bake for 30 minutes.

3. Uncover the pan and stir gently. Bake, uncovered, until browned, 30 minutes more. Let cool for 10 minutes before serving.

DEVILED EGGS WITH A TWIST

Deviled eggs are festive, traditional, and fun—and they look beautiful on a buffet table next to a ham. The "twist" here is the addition of smoked salmon, if you like. To save time, prepare the eggs well in advance. Just place the yolk mixture in a pastry bag, then refrigerate until ready to assemble the eggs. The smoked salmon adds an elegant, unexpected touch.

Serves 8

- 8 large eggs
- ½ cup chopped smoked salmon (about 2 ounces)
- ⅓ cup mayonnaise
- 1 tablespoon sweet pickle relish, plus 2 teaspoons relish liquid
- 2 teaspoons Dijon mustard or 1 teaspoon dry mustard
- Coarse salt
- Old Bay seasoning (optional), for garnish

1. In a large saucepan, cover the eggs with water and bring to a boil. Cover the pan, remove from the heat, and let stand for 10 minutes.

2. Gently drain the water from the pan. Run cold water over the eggs until chilled. Drain thoroughly, pat the eggs dry, and then peel them.

3. Cut the eggs in half lengthwise and carefully transfer the yolks to a medium nonreactive bowl. Using a fork, mash the yolks along with the salmon, mayonnaise, relish, relish juice, and mustard. Season to taste with salt. Using a pastry bag fitted with a small tip, mound the filling in the egg white halves and sprinkle with the Old Bay, if using. Chill the eggs slightly before serving, if you like.

GLAZED HAM

I was thrilled when my friend Kelly Alexander, a collaborator on this book, gave me two of her published cookbooks when she came to my house to test recipes. This is from her cookbook Peaches, *published by the UNC Press, and is a tried-and-true Southern classic.*

Serves 10 or more

One 10- to 12-pound smoked bone-in ham
   1 cup peach jelly
   1 cup firmly packed brown sugar
  ½ cup Dijon mustard
   2 teaspoons whole cloves

1. Position a rack in the center of the oven and preheat the oven to 300°F. Trim the tough outer skin and excess fat from the ham. Place the ham, meat-side down, in a large roasting pan and score the surface, making crosshatch incisions with a sharp knife. Roast for 1½ hours.

2. Remove the ham from the oven and increase the heat to 350°F. For the glaze, combine the peach jelly, brown sugar, and mustard in a medium bowl. Stud the exterior of the ham with the cloves (stick one clove at the intersection of each crosshatch), then brush the ham with the glaze and return to the oven.

3. Cook the ham for another hour, brushing it with more glaze at least three times. Transfer to a cutting board to rest for 20 minutes. Carve and serve warm or at room temperature.

SWEET-AND-SOUR CARROTS

This recipe is so easy to prepare and makes for such a colorful side dish for your ham buffet. I like to leave a little of the green tops on for a pretty presentation.

Serves 8

- 2½ pounds spring long baby carrots, peeled and green tops trimmed
- 1½ tablespoons extra-virgin olive oil
  Coarse salt and freshly ground pepper
- ½ cup red wine vinegar
- 1½ tablespoons sugar

1. Position a rack in the center of the oven and preheat the oven to 425°F.

2. Toss the carrots with the oil and season with salt and pepper and transfer to a large rimmed baking sheet. Roast for 10 minutes, rotate the pan and give the carrots a gentle shake, then roast until the carrots are barely tender, about 10 minutes longer.

3. In a small bowl, whisk the vinegar and sugar until the sugar has dissolved. Remove the carrots from the oven and drizzle the vinegar mixture over the carrots. Shake the baking sheet to coat them evenly. Return the carrots to the oven and continue to roast until the carrots are tender and the vinegar has evaporated, 5 to 8 minutes more. Serve on a large warmed platter.

LEMON CUPCAKES

You can freeze these cupcakes for four hours or overnight before you ice them, which makes the process so much easier. Also note that if you prefer a cake to a cupcake, you can use this batter in a greased 10-cup Bundt cake pan with a beautiful result. Simply bake the cake for 55 to 60 minutes, cool completely on a wire rack, and then dust with confectioner's sugar just prior to serving.

Makes 24 cupcakes

FOR THE CUPCAKES

- 3 cups all-purpose flour
- 2 teaspoons baking powder
- ½ teaspoon salt
- 8 tablespoons (1 stick) unsalted butter, softened
- 1½ cups sugar
- Finely grated zest of 2 lemons (about 2 tablespoons)
- ⅓ cup lemon juice
- 1 teaspoon vanilla extract
- 4 large eggs, lightly beaten
- 1 cup buttermilk

FOR THE LEMON CREAM FROSTING

- 12 ounces cream cheese, softened
- One 10-ounce jar lemon curd
- Fresh daisies (optional), for garnish
- Confectioner's sugar (optional), for garnish

1. **TO MAKE THE CUPCAKES:** Position the rack in the middle of the oven and preheat the oven to 375°F. Line a standard muffin pan with paper liners.

2. In a large bowl, sift together the flour, baking powder, and salt.

3. Combine the butter and the sugar in a medium bowl. Using an electric mixer, beat until light and fluffy and well combined, 3 to 5 minutes. Add the lemon zest, lemon juice, and vanilla and beat to combine. Slowly pour in the beaten eggs, a little at a time, beating well after each addition. Using a rubber spatula, scrape down the sides of the bowl as needed.

4. Slowly pour the butter-lemon mixture into the flour mixture in three additions, alternating with the buttermilk, beating thoroughly after each addition until the batter is smooth and without lumps.

5. Spoon the batter into the prepared pan and bake until a toothpick inserted into the center of a cupcake comes out clean, about 20 minutes. Transfer the pan to wire racks to cool completely before removing the cupcakes. (Cupcakes can be stored overnight at room temperature, or frozen up to 2 months, in airtight containers.)

6. **TO MAKE THE LEMON CREAM FROSTING:** In a medium bowl, using an electric mixer, beat the cream cheese until smooth. Add the lemon curd and beat well to combine. The mixture should be fluffy.

7. Decorate the cupcakes by spreading some of the frosting on top of each and arranging them on a platter. Decorate the platter with fresh daisies and dust the top of the cupcakes with confectioner's sugar, if you like.

Leg of Lamb
Supper Menu

Asparagus Vinaigrette

Leg of Lamb Roasted with Herbs

Potatoes au Gratin

Strawberry and White Chocolate Pavlova

ASPARAGUS VINAIGRETTE

Spring is all about rebirth and renewal, and with the beautiful yellow color of the chopped egg on the bright green asparagus, this dish feels fresh and new every time you serve it. You can prepare it up to two days in advance by blanching the asparagus, placing the spears on a long platter, and covering tightly with plastic wrap. Refrigerater until you're ready to garnish with the vinaigrette and the chopped egg.

Serves 8

Coarse salt

4   bunches thin asparagus (about 4 pounds), peeled and trimmed

3   tablespoons white wine vinegar

1   teaspoon Dijon mustard

Pinch of sugar

Freshly ground pepper

6   tablespoons extra-virgin olive oil

1   small shallot, finely chopped (about 2 teaspoons)

2   large eggs, hard-boiled, peeled, and finely chopped

1. Prepare an ice-water bath in a large, shallow bowl; set aside. Bring a large pot of water to a boil. Add a generous amount of salt and the asparagus. Return to a boil, and cook until the asparagus is bright green and tender, about 3 minutes. Transfer to the ice bath to cool.

2. In a small bowl, whisk together the vinegar, mustard, and sugar. Season with a pinch each of salt and pepper. Whisk in the oil. Add the shallots and whisk to combine. Taste, and adjust the seasoning with more salt and pepper, if necessary.

3. Drain the asparagus well, then transfer to a serving platter. Drizzle the vinaigrette over the asparagus and then sprinkle with the chopped egg. Serve the dish immediately, or let stand at room temperature for up to 30 minutes before serving.

LEG OF LAMB ROASTED WITH HERBS

For decades I have been preparing this leg of lamb for our Easter feasts. Don't bother to trim the leg: that way you'll have the maximum surface area on which to spread the herb paste. I like to serve the whole leg in the center of a platter and slice it at the table.

Serves 8

One 7- to 8-pound leg of lamb, shank bone removed and tied

½ cup water

¼ cup extra-virgin olive oil

¼ cup balsamic vinegar

1 large red onion, thinly sliced (about ⅔ cup)

⅔ cup coarsely chopped fresh flat-leaf parsley

3 garlic cloves, minced

2 teaspoons dried oregano

1 teaspoon dried rosemary

1 large egg white

1 teaspoon coarse salt

¼ teaspoon freshly ground pepper

1. Wash the lamb and pat it dry with paper towels. If necessary, trim the fat layer to an even ¼-inch thickness all over the lamb. Place the lamb, meat-side down, in a large roasting pan and score the surface, making crosshatch incisions with a sharp knife. Place the lamb in a large roasting pan.

2. In a small bowl, whisk together the water, oil, and vinegar to make a marinade, then toss in the onion slices, stirring to combine. Pour the mixture over the lamb, cover, and refrigerate for at least 8 hours or overnight, turning the lamb occasionally to evenly distribute the marinade.

3. Position the rack in the center of the oven and preheat the oven to 325°F. Let the lamb come to room temperature by removing the lamb from the refrigerator 1 hour prior to roasting. Position the lamb fat-side up in the pan. Roast the lamb for 1½ hours.

4. Meanwhile, in the bowl of a food processor, combine the parsley, garlic, oregano, and rosemary, and pulse until finely chopped, 4 or 5 pulses. Add the egg white, salt, and pepper, and process until the mixture forms a paste.

5. Remove the lamb from the oven. With a butter knife, fill the scored lines with the herb paste. Return the lamb to the oven and roast until an instant-read thermometer inserted into the thickest part of the center of the roast reaches 140°F for medium rare, about 30 minutes. Transfer the lamb to a carving board to rest for 10 minutes, loosely covered with foil. Slice the lamb and serve on a warmed platter garnished with spring greens, if you like.

POTATOES AU GRATIN

This recipe is designed to be prepared the day before your festive meal, giving you one less thing to do on the big day. I love leeks, so I sometimes combine them with the potatoes before baking the gratin, and I encourage you to give it a try, too. You might also try a two-potato gratin: substitute sweet potatoes for half of the russets.

Serves 8

- 3 pounds medium russet potatoes, peeled and thinly sliced
- 2 cups whole milk
- 2 cups water
- 3 garlic cloves, minced
- Coarse salt
- 3 bay leaves
- 1 tablespoon unsalted butter, softened
- 1 cup heavy cream
- 10 ounces Gruyère cheese, shredded
- Freshly ground nutmeg
- Freshly ground pepper

1. Position a rack in the center of the oven and preheat the oven to 375°F. Lightly butter a shallow 2½-quart gratin or casserole dish.

2. Place the potato slices in a large heavy stockpot and then add the milk and water. Add the garlic, a little salt, and the bay leaves. Bring to a boil over medium-high heat, partially covered, stirring occasionally to prevent the potatoes from sticking to the bottom of the pot. Cook until the potatoes are tender but not falling apart, 10 to 15 minutes.

3. Drain the potatoes in a colander. Discard the bay leaves.

4. Using a slotted spoon, transfer half of the potatoes to the prepared pan. Add the butter, drizzle with ½ cup of the cream, sprinkle half of the cheese over the potatoes, and then season with nutmeg and pepper to taste.

5. Cover with the remaining potatoes and add the remaining ½ cup cream, the cheese, and nutmeg and pepper to taste. Bake the gratin until the potatoes on top are crisp and golden, about 1 hour. Remove the gratin from the oven, cover loosely with foil, and let rest for 10 minutes before serving.

Strawberry and White Chocolate Pavlova

What's great about a pavlova is that you can make the meringue shell a day in advance and then "garnish" it with the fruit filling before serving. The finished pavlova looks somewhat like a frosted cake.

Serves 8

For the Meringue

- 6 large egg whites, at room temperature
- 1 teaspoon cream of tartar
- 2 cups superfine sugar
- 1 tablespoon apple cider vinegar

For Assembling the Pavlova

- 2 cups heavy cream
- 20 fresh strawberries (about 12 ounces), hulled and halved
- 2 ounces white chocolate

1. **TO MAKE THE MERINGUE:** Preheat the oven to 300°F and line a baking sheet with parchment. Using a 9-inch round cake pan as a guide, trace a circle on the paper with a pencil. Flip the paper over so your meringue will not touch the pencil marks—you will still be able to see the circle.

2. In the bowl of a standing mixer fitted with a whisk, beat the egg whites with the cream of tartar at medium speed until soft peaks form. Raise the speed to medium-high and then gradually beat in the sugar, a tablespoon at a time, until the meringue is stiff, glossy, and firm, about 10 minutes. Fold in the vinegar. Secure the parchment to the baking sheet with a dab of meringue under each corner. Using your circle drawing as a guide, use a large spoon to dollop and mound the meringue onto the parchment within the circle, smoothing the sides and the top with a spatula.

3. Bake until the meringue is crisp and dry on top, but still a little loose in the center, about 1 hour and 10 minutes. Turn off the oven and open the door slightly, and let the meringue disk cool completely in the oven.

4. Once cool, use a spatula to transfer the pavlova from the baking sheet onto a big flat-bottomed plate, gently peeling it off the parchment. You may make the pavlova one day ahead up to this point. To store the meringue shell, gently wrap it in plastic and store in a cool dry place.

5. **TO ASSEMBLE THE PAVLOVA:** Using an electric mixer fitted with a chilled wire whisk, whip the cream until thick but still soft, about 5 minutes. Pile the whipped cream on top of the meringue, then scatter the strawberries on top.

6. Coarsely grate or shave the white chocolate over the top to decorate, taking care not to cover up the fruit.

Roast Beef Supper Menu

Yorkshire Popovers

Standing Rib Roast

Red Wine Mushroom Sauce

Crunchy Bones

Chocolate Pots de Crème

YORKSHIRE POPOVERS

I grew up eating this traditional English accompaniment to roasts—not least because my family is from England. When I was young, I was allowed to help whisk the batter from time to time and it was my pleasure to do as I was told. Now that I am an adult, I like to prepare the batter in a food processor—it sure cuts down on prep time.

Serves 8

- 6 large eggs, at room temperature
- 1½ cups all-purpose flour
- ½ teaspoon coarse salt
- 1 teaspoon freshly ground pepper
- 2 cups whole milk, at room temperature
- 2 tablespoons unsalted butter, cut into ¼-inch pats

1. Position a rack in the center of the oven and preheat the oven to 400°F.

2. In a food processor, combine the eggs, flour, salt, and pepper. Blend until thoroughly combined, about 1 minute. Gradually add the milk and blend until the mixture has bubbles on the top layer, about 3 minutes more.

3. In a jumbo muffin pan, place one pat of butter into each muffin cup. Place the tin in the oven until the butter melts and becomes very, very hot and almost smoking, about 5 minutes. Carefully and quickly pour the batter into the muffin cups, filling each about three-quarters full.

4. Bake until puffed and golden brown, 20 to 25 minutes. Do not open the oven door. Remove the popovers from the muffin pan and cool slightly on a wire rack. Serve warm.

NOTE
Prepare this recipe while the Standing Rib Roast is resting.

STANDING RIB ROAST

This elegant but simple roast will make your whole house smell terrific—rich and intense—and draw your meat eaters right into the kitchen. I like to ask my butcher to remove the rib bones from the roast and then re-tie them on so I can prepare the crunchy bones, an often-discarded part of a roast that I find worth making use of—give it a try. (These crunchy bones happen to be my personal favorite.)

Serves 8

One 8- to 9-pound standing rib roast of beef, rib bones removed

Extra-virgin olive oil, for coating

Coarse salt and freshly ground pepper

4 teaspoons dried thyme

1. Wash the roast and pat it dry with paper towels. Place the roast, fat-side up, on a wire rack set inside a large, deep roasting pan. Rub the roast all over with oil, salt, pepper, and the thyme. Let stand at room temperature for 2 hours.

2. Meanwhile, place a rack in the lower third of the oven and preheat the oven to 500°F. Roast for 15 minutes to give the outside of the roast a good brown crust, then lower the heat to 325°F. Roast until an instant-read thermometer inserted into the thickest part of the center of the roast reads 140°F for medium-rare, about 3 hours.

3. When the roast is done, transfer it to a carving board and cover loosely with foil to rest while you prepare the Red Wine Mushroom Sauce, Crunchy Bones, and Yorkshire Popovers.

RED WINE MUSHROOM SAUCE

After you enjoy this savory sauce with your roasted supper, I encourage you to use any leftovers to make your own easy version of Beef Stroganoff (page 43): Slice the remaining roast beef, combine it in a skillet with this sauce and a little sour cream (add more mushrooms, if you like), then serve it over buttered egg noodles and with a simple salad for a quick weeknight supper.

Makes about 4 cups sauce

- 2 tablespoons unsalted butter
- 2 large shallots, finely chopped (about ½ cup)
- 2 pounds baby bella mushrooms, halved
  Coarse salt and freshly ground pepper
- 1 teaspoon dried thyme
- 1 bay leaf
- 1½ teaspoons all-purpose flour
- 2 cups dry red wine
- 2 cups beef broth, homemade or store-bought

In a medium saucepan over low heat, melt the butter. Add the shallots and cook, stirring, until soft, 8 to 10 minutes. Add the mushrooms and continue to cook until soft, about 8 minutes more. Season with salt and pepper and add the thyme and bay leaf. Stir in the flour and cook, stirring constantly, for another minute to incorporate. Gradually whisk in the wine and continue to cook, whisking constantly, until smooth and incorporated, about 15 minutes. Whisk in the broth, reduce the heat to a low simmer, and cook until reduced by half, about 1 hour. Whisk in any of the roast's accumulated juices from the cutting board and cook until warmed through. Remove the bay leaf. Keep the gravy warm until ready to serve, then ladle into a warmed gravy boat and pass with the roast.

CRUNCHY BONES

Here are my famous crunchy bones—and I promise your family will love this recipe as much as mine does. If you have young children and have a hard time getting them to eat meat, tell them these are "tyrannosaurus bones" and watch them dig in. (It works for the big guys, too.)

Serves 8

- 6 to 7 cooked standing rib roast bones, cut in between the joints to make individual pieces
- ¾ cup Dijon mustard
- ¼ cup Worcestershire sauce
- ¼ cup soy sauce
- 9 garlic cloves, minced
- ½ teaspoon dried thyme

Place a rack in the upper third of the oven and preheat the oven to 425°F. Place the bones on a baking sheet in a single layer. In a small saucepan over medium-high heat, combine the rest of the ingredients. Whisking to combine, bring the mixture just to a boil and then remove it from the heat. Using a kitchen brush, paint the sauce generously on the ribs. Bake the bones until golden brown and crispy, 20 to 25 minutes. Serve alongside the roast beef on a large warmed platter.

CHOCOLATE POTS DE CRÈME

Chocolate is the perfect finishing touch to this roast supper. Here the pots de crème, a French dessert named for the little ramekins that hold the custards, are not only rich and indulgent—they're also a time-saver because you can make them as early as two days in advance and refrigerate until ready to eat.

Serves 8

- 8 ounces semisweet chocolate, finely chopped
- ⅓ cup hot strong coffee
- 4 large eggs, separated
- Coarse salt
- Whipped cream (optional), for serving
- Grated chocolate (optional), for serving

1. Chill a large nonreactive bowl for 30 minutes.

2. Place the chocolate, coffee, and egg yolks in a blender and blend thoroughly. Transfer the chocolate mixture to a large bowl.

3. In a large chilled bowl, using a hand mixer, beat the egg whites with a pinch of salt until stiff. Gently fold the egg whites into the chocolate mixture until thoroughly combined, taking care not to overmix.

4. Divide the mixture evenly between 8 small ramekins. Cover each with plastic wrap and refrigerate for at least 3 hours or overnight, or up to 2 days.

5. To serve, garnish with whipped cream and grated chocolate, if you like.

ROAST TURKEY
SUPPER MENU

Roasted Brussels Sprouts with Balsamic Vinegar

Roasted Turkey

Giblet Gravy

Sweet Potato Wedges

Cranberry-Orange Relish

Pecan Squares

ROASTED BRUSSELS SPROUTS
WITH BALSAMIC VINEGAR

These sprouts are perfect as they are, but if you'd like to add a little more interest and crunch to them, simply toss some finely diced prosciutto onto the baking pan while the sprouts are roasting.

Serves 8

- 2½ pounds Brussels sprouts, tough outer leaves removed and stems trimmed
- 3½ tablespoons extra-virgin olive oil
- 2½ tablespoons lemon juice
  Coarse salt and freshly ground pepper
- 2 tablespoons balsamic vinegar

1. Position racks in the upper and lower thirds of the oven and pre-heat the oven to 425°F.

2. Use a serrated knife to cut each sprout in half lengthwise.

3. In a large bowl, toss the sprouts with the oil and lemon juice. Season with salt and pepper and turn them out onto two baking sheets, arranging them cut-sides down. Roast in the upper and lower thirds of the oven for 20 minutes, rotating the pans and switching them from top to bottom halfway through the cooking time, until the sprouts are just tender and nicely browned on the bottom.

4. Transfer the sprouts to a large bowl, drizzle with the vinegar, and serve immediately.

ROASTED TURKEY

The more frequently you roast a turkey on a night that isn't Thanksgiving, the easier it's going to be on the big day—practice makes perfect. And the bonus of roasting a turkey is that you get great leftovers; my family loves using them to make Turkey Tetrazzini (page 109).

Serves 10

One 12- to 14-pound whole turkey, preferably organic, neck saved for gravy

4 tablespoons (½ stick) unsalted butter, softened

4 tablespoons margarine

½ cup poultry seasoning

2 tablespoons coarse salt

2 tablespoons smoked paprika

Fresh sage leaves and thyme sprigs

1. Wash the turkey inside and out with cool water. Drain it well and pat dry all over with paper towels. Lay the bird on top of a rack positioned in a large roasting pan. Rub the turkey all over with the butter and margarine to coat well. In a small bowl, combine the poultry seasoning, salt, and paprika. Rub the spice mixture all over the turkey, inside and out. Place the sage and thyme deep inside the turkey's cavity. Tie the legs together with kitchen twine and tie the wings close to the body. Cover loosely with aluminum foil and refrigerate until ready to roast, at least 8 hours or overnight.

2. One hour before roasting the turkey, remove it from the refrigerator, take off the aluminum foil, and allow it to come to room temperature. Position a rack on the lowest rung in the oven and preheat the oven to 450°F.

3. Position the roasting pan in the oven turkey legs first and roast for 45 minutes, or until the turkey begins to get a nice golden color on the skin. Lower the temperature to 325°F and roast for another 3 to 3½ hours, basting every hour with the pan juices. The turkey is done when an instant-read thermometer inserted into the thickest part of the thigh (careful not to touch the bone) registers 165°F and the juices run clear with no hint of pink when pierced with a knife.

4. Transfer the turkey to a carving board and loosely cover it with aluminum foil. Let the turkey rest for up to 30 minutes before carving.

GIBLET GRAVY

The great thing about this gravy is that it doesn't depend on the turkey; you can get the turkey necks from a butcher, prepare the gravy several days prior to serving, and then gently rewarm it over low heat, adjusting the seasonings to taste.

Makes about 6 cups

- 3 turkey necks
- 2 quarts (8 cups) water
- 2 medium celery stalks, coarsely chopped (about 1 cup)
- 1 small yellow onion, coarsely chopped (about ⅔ cup)
- 1 teaspoon coarse salt, plus more to taste
- ⅓ cup all-purpose flour
- 2 cups chicken broth, homemade or store-bought
- Freshly ground pepper

1. In a large, heavy saucepan, cover the necks with the water and add the celery, onion, and salt. Over medium-high heat, bring the mixture to a boil; reduce the heat to low and simmer for 1 hour. Remove the pan from the heat and let the liquid stand until cool, about 20 minutes. You should have about 6 cups liquid. If you have more than 6 cups of liquid, simmer to reduce it to 6 cups.

2. Strain the cooking liquid through a fine mesh strainer into a small saucepan. Using your hands, pick the meat off the necks and then use a knife to finely chop the meat. Add the neck meat to the strained cooking liquid. Set the saucepan over medium heat, stir in the flour, and cook, stirring constantly, until the mixture darkens to golden, about 3 minutes. Gradually add the broth, whisking until the gravy is thick and smooth, with no floury lumps. Taste and adjust the seasoning with salt and pepper.

SWEET POTATO WEDGES

From the kitchen of Sarah Smothers

This recipe, which offers a traditional turkey side dish with a twist, was devised by our daughter Sarah. What I love is that it takes advantage of the hot oven after roasting the turkey and can be made while the bird rests.

Serves 8

Nonstick cooking spray

6 medium sweet potatoes (2 to 2½ pounds)

¼ cup extra-virgin olive oil

2 tablespoons fresh rosemary, torn, or 2 teaspoons dried

1 tablespoon fresh thyme, coarsely chopped, or 1 teaspoon dried

1 teaspoon coarse salt

1. Preheat the oven to 400°F. Coat a large, heavy baking sheet with nonstick cooking spray.

2. Peel the sweet potatoes and cut them first in half lengthwise and then into 1-inch wedges. In a large bowl, toss the sweet potatoes with the oil, rosemary, thyme, and salt until evenly coated.

3. Spread the wedges out on the prepared baking sheet and roast, turning every 10 minutes, until browned and tender, 40 to 45 minutes. Serve in a large rimmed serving dish.

CRANBERRY-ORANGE RELISH

This simple, fresh relish is excellent on leftover turkey sandwiches and can also be used to perk up other weeknight meals—it's great alongside grilled chicken breasts or lamb chops.

Serves 8

1 large navel orange

One 12-ounce bag fresh cranberries

2 tablespoons raw local honey

1 tablespoon sugar

Pinch of coarse salt

1. Grate 2 teaspoons zest from the orange. Remove and discard the remaining peel and pith. Holding the orange over a bowl, cut between the membranes, allowing the segments and juice to fall into the bowl. Squeeze the juice from the membranes into the bowl; discard the membranes. Slice the segments crosswise. Add the zest to the bowl.

2. Pulse half the cranberries in a food processor until finely chopped. Add the remaining cranberries, and pulse just until the second addition is coarsely chopped. Add the cranberries to the orange segments and zest along with the honey, sugar, and salt, and gently combine. Cover and refrigerate overnight or up to 2 weeks. Serve chilled or at room temperature.

PECAN SQUARES

Not only am I well known among my friends for these little pecan squares, but they also happen to be Chris's favorite dessert. I usually make a double batch because he and our children like to put these squares in the freezer to enjoy all winter long. Don't bother counting calories here!

Serves 8

FOR THE CRUST

- 1 pound (4 sticks) unsalted butter, softened
- 4 cups all-purpose flour
- 1 cup confectioner's sugar
- 1 teaspoon salt

FOR THE FILLING

- 4 cups pecan halves
- 2 cups light corn syrup
- 2 cups sugar
- 6 large eggs, lightly beaten
- 4 tablespoons (½ stick) unsalted butter, softened
- 2 teaspoons vanilla extract

1. **TO MAKE THE CRUST:** Preheat the oven to 350°F.

2. In the bowl of a large standing mixer, using the whisk attachment, whip 2 cups of the butter until smooth. Add the flour, confectioner's sugar, and salt and mix on medium speed until thoroughly combined and crumbs form, about 4 minutes. Scrape the dough out of the bowl onto a clean work surface and, using your hands, gently form the dough into a large ball.

3. Place the ball in the center of a large baking sheet. Using your hands, spread the dough out over the bottom of the pan in an even layer about ½ inch thick. Prick the dough with a fork several times all over. Bake until the crust begins to brown, 20 to 25 minutes. Let the crust cool completely while you make the filling.

4. **TO MAKE THE FILLING:** In a large bowl, mix the pecan halves, corn syrup, sugar, eggs, butter, and vanilla. Pour over the crust. Bake until a toothpick inserted into the filling comes out clean, about 1 hour. Transfer the pan to a rack to cool completely, then cut into squares of desired size and serve at room temperature.

TIP
To make these treats even more indulgent and intense, add 1 cup dark chocolate morsels to the filling.

Southern "Not Fried" Chicken Supper Menu

Collard Greens with Caramelized Leeks

Buttermilk "Not Fried" Chicken

Triple-Berry Cobbler

Skillet-Fresh Corn

COLLARD GREENS WITH CARAMELIZED LEEKS

This traditional southern side gets an update courtesy of the leeks and the dark ale, both of which add complexity to the smoky greens and bacon. I recommend Samuel Smith's Nut Brown Ale, Newcastle Brown Ale, Brooklyn Brown Ale, or any favorite brown beer.

Serves 8

- 2 tablespoons extra-virgin olive oil
- 4 garlic cloves, minced
- ½ teaspoon crushed red pepper flakes
  Coarse salt and freshly ground pepper
- 4 pounds collard greens, trimmed and tough center stems removed, cut into 2-inch strips
- 4½ cups chicken broth, homemade or store-bought
- ½ cup apple cider vinegar
- 1 tablespoon sugar
- One 12-ounce bottle good brown beer or 12 ounces water or chicken broth
- ½ pound center-cut thick bacon (about 5 slices), diced
- 4 large leeks, white and tender green parts only, thinly sliced (about 3 cups)

1. In a 9-quart stockpot, heat the oil over medium-high heat. Add the garlic and red pepper flakes and cook, stirring, until fragrant, about 1 minute. Season to taste with salt and pepper. Stir in the greens, broth, vinegar, and sugar. Add the beer. Bring to a boil, then reduce the heat to medium for a low simmer. Cook, uncovered, until the greens are tender, about 2 hours.

2. Meanwhile, in a medium skillet over medium-high heat, cook the bacon until crisp, about 15 minutes. Set aside to drain on a paper towel-lined plate. Remove all but 1 tablespoon of the bacon drippings from the skillet. Add the leeks, reduce the heat to low, and cook until golden and caramelized, 20 to 25 minutes.

3. Transfer the greens to a large casserole. Top with the bacon and caramelized leeks. Serve immediately.

BUTTERMILK "NOT FRIED" CHICKEN

I first wrote about this healthier alternative to fried chicken in my cookbook Mr. Sunday's Saturday Night Chicken, *and my readers were so pleasantly surprised at how crisp and addictive it is that I've decided to share it again—it's too good to file in the archives. The buttermilk bath and the herbs also help give the chicken its addictive moistness and tangy flavor.*

Serves 8

Two 3½- to 4-pound chickens, each cut into
8 pieces

4 cups buttermilk

4 garlic cloves, crushed

2 teaspoons dried rosemary

2 teaspoons dried marjoram

2 teaspoons dried sage

2 teaspoons dried thyme

1½ teaspoons coarse salt

1 teaspoon cayenne pepper
Nonstick cooking spray

8 cups cornflakes cereal, finely crushed
Coarse salt and freshly ground pepper

8 tablespoons (1 stick) unsalted butter, melted

1. Rinse the chicken pieces with cold water and pat dry with paper towels.

2. In a large bowl, stir together the buttermilk, garlic, rosemary, marjoram, sage, thyme, salt, and cayenne. Add the chicken and turn to coat well. Cover and refrigerate for up to 4 hours or overnight.

3. Preheat the oven to 350°F. Line two baking sheets with aluminum foil and then coat with nonstick cooking spray. Remove the chicken from the refrigerator and let stand at room temperature for 30 minutes.

4. Place the crushed cornflakes in a shallow dish and sprinkle with a pinch each of salt and pepper. Roll the chicken pieces in the cornflakes to coat and set on the prepared baking sheets. Bake the chicken for 15 minutes, then rotate the baking sheets and switch onto alternate racks. Drizzle with the melted butter. Continue to bake until golden brown and cooked through, about 45 minutes more. Serve piled on a large platter.

TRIPLE-BERRY COBBLER

Cobbler is the ultimate easy summer dessert: It's a like a pie but without the bother of having to make a traditional crust. The tart-tangy berries are made sweeter by the buttery biscuitlike topping, and you can garnish the cobbler with whipped cream or any favorite ice cream—cinnamon ice cream is particularly good with this recipe.

Serves 8

- 2 cups fresh or thawed frozen blueberries
- 1 cup fresh or thawed frozen raspberries
- 1 cup fresh or thawed frozen blackberries
- 1 cup plus 1 tablespoon granulated sugar
- 1 tablespoon cornstarch
- 2 tablespoons water
- 2 cups all-purpose flour
- ½ cup lightly packed light brown sugar
- 8 tablespoons (1 stick) unsalted butter, cut into small pieces
- 2 teaspoons ground cinnamon

1. Preheat the oven to 375°F.

2. Place the berries and ½ cup of the granulated sugar in a medium saucepan and bring to a boil over medium-high heat. Meanwhile, mix together the cornstarch and water in a small bowl, then add to the berries and cook, stirring, for 1 minute. Transfer the berries and thickened juices into a 1½- to 2-quart baking dish or casserole dish and set aside.

3. Sift together the flour, ½ cup of the granulated sugar, and the brown sugar in a medium mixing bowl. Using a pastry cutter or two knives, work the butter into the flour until it resembles coarse meal. Spread the topping evenly over the berry filling and pat down firmly with the palms of your hands and your fingers, smoothing out the top. Sprinkle the topping with the remaining 1 tablespoon granulated sugar and the cinnamon.

4. Bake until the crust is golden brown and bubbly, about 40 minutes. Set aside to cool briefly before serving with whipped cream or vanilla or cinnamon ice cream (or both).

SKILLET-FRESH CORN

If you can't find truly fresh sweet corn, simply add a pinch of sugar to the skillet to approximate that "fresh off the cob" taste. After cutting the corn from the cob, extract the juice from the cob by pressing it with the dull side of a knife, and then add the juice to the kernels.

Serves 8

- 12 ears corn, kernels cut from the cob (about 3 cups) and juice extracted from the cobs
- 2 tablespoons unsalted butter
- ½ cup half-and-half
- 1 teaspoon coarse salt
- ½ teaspoon freshly ground pepper

1. Hold each ear of corn upright in a large bowl and use a sharp knife to cut the kernels from the cobs into the bowl. With the dull side of the knife, press down along the length of each cob to extract the corn's liquid, and add that to the cut corn.

2. In a large cast-iron skillet over medium-high heat, melt the butter until it begins to foam. Add the corn and corn juice, stir to combine, and continue to cook for about 5 minutes. Add the half-and-half and stir into the corn. Add the salt and pepper and continue to cook until heated thoroughly, 6 to 8 minutes longer. Serve from the skillet or transfer to a warmed serving bowl and serve immediately.